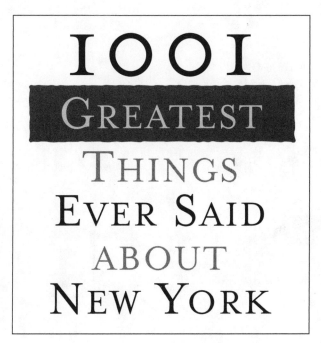

# 1001
## GREATEST
## THINGS
## EVER SAID
## ABOUT
## NEW YORK

# 1001
## GREATEST
## THINGS
## EVER SAID
## ABOUT
## NEW YORK

Edited and with an Introduction by

C. J. Sullivan

THE LYONS PRESS
Guilford, Connecticut
An imprint of The Globe Pequot Press

The Lyons Press is an imprint of The Globe Pequot Press.

10 9 8 7 6 5 4 3 2 1

Printed in the United States of America

Designed by Carol Sawyer/Rose Design

ISBN-13: 978-1-59228-997-4

ISBN-10: 1-59228-997-5

Library of Congress Cataloging-in-Publication Data is available on file.

*This is dedicated to my parents, Lt. William Sullivan, FDNY, and Kathleen Sullivan. Thank you for giving me the gift of New York City. I am passing that down to my children, Luisa M. Sullivan and Olivia K. Sullivan.*

*To all the people who built this city and kept it from burning down.*

# CONTENTS

New York is the perfect model of a city, not the model of a perfect city.

—*Lewis Mumford*

# ACKNOWLEDGMENTS

I've needed a lot of help, and every time I reached out someone was there with a strong grip to pull me up. I only hope I have been there as much for you.

I want to thank my family. I would not be where I am without you.

Praise to Scott Bowen and Holly Rubino of The Lyons Press for reaching out to me to do this wonderful project.

I want to thank all my editors, past and present, at the New York Press for giving me a shot at journalism.

The *New York Post* has been my rock and solace for the last two years, and a real big bow of gratitude goes to "Captain" Billy Gorta, Keith Kelly, Michelle Gothelff, Jesse Angelo, and Kate Sheehy. You all cover New York like no other newspaper and have made me a better journalist for working with you. Thanks for that and all the stories.

I want to thank Cynthia Ceilan for her help and inspiration with this project. At times you saw it better than I did.

A BIG thank you to all my New York State Court friends. The Senior Court Clerks of Brooklyn Supreme Court whom I have represented for the last ten years rule. You all have been there for me for over seventeen years. You are too numerous to mention but know I appreciate you all—well most of you.

I can't forget my Bronx crew of Steve Geary, Ed Hefele, Ed Steffens, David McGlynn, Jim Cannon, Mannix, and Kevin Sheerin.

Thanks to Aunt Marcella, Mary, Tom, Kathleen, and Ann MacClave and Kathleen, Rose, and Billy Sullivan.

A thank you to Lisa for doing a great job with Olivia and Luisa.

# INTRODUCTION

*N*o one person can ever know New York City—at least not in
full. Thomas Wolfe claimed that only the dead know Brooklyn, which
is only one of New York's five boroughs. New York is *the* Big City, not
just in America but maybe the world. It is a hard city to capture because it is always in flux. New York is a living, breathing Colossus that
is forever changing.

I am a native New Yorker and have spent my entire life in this
Shining City. The longer I live here the more I find out all the things I
don't know about it. The obvious missed in my daily travels. The
things that hide in plain sight. And that is the joy—and sometimes
the despair—of New York City.

So to take on a project entitled *1001 Greatest Things Ever Said about
New York* was daunting. Is there a finite number of greatest quotes?
And why one quote and not another? Like an irrepressible cock-eyed
optimist, I jumped right in by invoking a little "Amazin' " New York

Met mojo with the help of Casey Stengel's spirit: "Wake up muscles. We're in New York now."

The trick was to re-create the city as it was and is today—to give a voice to all aspects of this teeming metropolis. I tried to capture the history and the ever-changing present. And I had to be quick about it. You stand too long in the same place in New York City and they'll pave right over you. The quotes that follow are as diverse as New York itself and most of them will be new to even the most seasoned reader. There are a few legendary voices here, like Jimmy Breslin, Langston Hughes, and Joan Didion, but the book opens up new angles. Listen to what Lil' Kim, Billy Gorta, Cindy Ramos, Colson Whitehead, and Steve Geary have to say. Some of the most poignant quotes I got from working at the *New York Post* and listening to the wisdom from street corner philosophers. There were things said that cleared my head like a March wind. You have to stay current in New York because this city isn't called "New" York for nothing.

"The only credential the city asked was the boldness to dream," Moss Hart once said. As a kid growing up in the Bronx I dreamed about having my name on the cover of a book. Call it a dream deferred because of self-doubt. I grew up three blocks from Edgar Allan Poe's cottage on East Kingsbridge Road. While visiting his former abode, I used to glare at the ominous, black, stuffed raven in his parlor thinking that the life of a writer was beyond my station in the pecking order of the work world of New York.

But that was then. And this is now. With this book I get to bring to you what scores of people have said about New York. Open it to any page and a voice will hit you about what makes this city the dream of America.

This book is part of my American Dream. And New York has always been a big part of what the world thinks of when it thinks of the America Dream. It is still this nation's port of entry. The dreams I had about doing a book came true because I believed that if I hung in there in New York long enough all my dreams would come true. After all, I had been surrounded by Frank Sinatra's declaration, "If I can make it there, I'll make it anywhere . . ." all my life.

I hope I was bold enough to dare to capture this elusive city. Whether I've succeeded is for you to judge. No matter where you call home, I hope this book satisfies your "inner" New Yorker.

# BUILDINGS,
# BRIDGES,
# TUNNELS,
# SKY

A mighty woman with a torch, whose flame is the imprisoned lightning, and her name is Mother of Exiles.
        —*Emma Lazarus on the Statue of Liberty*

Up and down along and between Lenox and Seventh and Eighth Avenue, Harlem was like some Technicolor bazaar.
        —*Malcolm X*

. . . the blind skyscrapers use their full height to proclaim the strength of Collective Man.
        —*W. H. Auden on the majesty of the New York skyline*

About the only Queen this city has really ever had is the Statue of Liberty.

—*Liz Smith*

How often I have had Manhattan described to me from these bridges! They tell me the view is loveliest in the morning and at sunset when one sees the skyscrapers rising like fairy palaces.

—*Helen Keller*

Walking across the Brooklyn Bridge was like walking into an enormous spider web.

—*Mary Cantwell*

Park Avenue has the essence of a pen-and-ink drawing of Paris.
*—Zelda Fitzgerald*

New York is a vertical town. The emphasis is on things that rise.
*—Thomas Beller*

Mighty Manhattan with spires, and the sparkling and hurrying tides.
*—Walt Whitman on viewing*
*Manhattan from the East River*

There's a right and a wrong side of the tracks in every city; but in
New York what floor you live on, which direction your apartment
faces says a tremendous amount about who you are.

—*Steven Gaines*

People on Lexington Avenue are wishing that they lived in a more
cheerful street.
   —*Edmund Wilson on the banality of Lexington Avenue compared
       to the more glamorous Park, Madison, and Fifth Avenues*

As one comes down the Henry Hudson Parkway along the river in
the dusk, New York is never real; it is always fabulous.

—*Anthony Bailey*

One green wave moved in the violet sea like the UN building on big evenings, green and wet while the sky turns violet.

—*James Schuyler*

We watched the world go home that night
In a flood through Union Square . . .

—*Sara Teasdale*

It was the towers of Manhattan one wanted to see suddenly garlanded with loveliness. One wanted life for them and for oneself together.

—*Paul Rosenfeld*

I often feel drawn to the Hudson River. It hypnotizes me.
—*Joseph Mitchell*

~

There are two things I hear—and am aware that I live in the
neighborhood of—the roar of the sea and the hum of the city.
—*Henry David Thoreau while living*
*on Staten Island in 1843*

~

This bridge is such a sublime vantage, with its cold steel framework
and harsh glare, a snowy Olympus over New York.
—*L. B. Deyo on the George Washington Bridge*

~

The New Yorker's panic-stricken need for accomplishment is matched by a kind of vertigo that comes with being constantly aware of the distance below.

—*Thomas Beller*

Down by the waterfront, an unreconstructed house of sex, drugs, and violence fights City Hall. Its weapons are its obscure address and a decent Court Street lawyer.

—*Michael Brick on a strip club in Brooklyn*

Yet the speakeasy pervades Manhattan with a fascinating atmosphere of mystery.

—*Paul Morand*

One day a miracle should happen over the magnificent harbor, and set life thrilling and rhythming through the place of New York.

—*Paul Rosenfeld*

Broadway is a main artery of New York life—the hardened artery.

—*Walter Winchell*

New Yorkers are nice about giving directions; in fact, they seem proud of knowing where they are themselves.

—*Katherine Bush*

New York is the greatest place where the lights meet the road.

—*G. N. Miller*

Traffic signals in New York are just rough guidelines.
*—David Letterman*

New York City is a great monument to the power of money and greed . . . a race for rent.
*—Frank Lloyd Wright*

New York is the perfect model of a city, not the model of a perfect city.
*—Lewis Mumford*

The World Trade Center symbolized New York's extraordinary present, dense past, and apparently limitless future.

*—Pete Hamill*

❧

When I was living in New York and didn't have a penny to my name, I would walk around the streets and occasionally I would see an alcove. . . . And I'd think . . . that'll be a good spot for me when I'm homeless.

*—Larry David*

❧

. . . skyscrapers are the last word of economic ingenuity only till another word be written.

*—Henry James*

❧

Holy the solitudes of skyscrapers and pavements! Holy the cafeteria filled with millions! Holy the mysterious river of tears under the streets! . . . Holy New York . . .

*—Allen Ginsberg*

New York is a granite beehive, where people jostle and whiz like molecules in an overheated jar.

*—Nigel Goslin*

The rose-colored towers of New York appear, a vision whose harshness is mitigated by distance.

*—Le Corbusier*

As black and resolute as a subway train, we raced down a corridor.
*—Louis-Ferdinand Celine*

Beginning in the pool of glass that covers the Grand Central tracks,
Park Avenue flows quietly and smoothly up Manhattan.
*—Zelda Fitzgerald*

New York is the great stone desert.
*—Israel Zangwill*

New York . . . is a city of geometric heights, a petrified desert of grids and lattices, an inferno of greenish abstraction under a flat sky, a real Metropolis from which man is absent by his very accumulation.

*—Roland Barthes*

Silent, grim, colossal, the Big City has ever stood against its revilers.

*—O. Henry*

Fifth Avenue will always be the street against which all others will be measured.

*—Steven Gaines*

[New York] is to the nation what the white church spire is to the village—the visible symbol of aspiration and faith, the white plume saying the way is up.

*—E. B. White*

Then it is almost beauty that comes to dress the slipshod harbor of New York.

*—Paul Rosenfeld*

. . . being a city kid, I was slow to appreciate the impact of nature on those raised differently.

*—George Sheehan*

I have never walked down Fifth Avenue alone without thinking of money.

—*Anthony Trollope*

New York was to be the city of skyscrapers, a man-made Rocky Mountain range wondrous to behold.

—*Edward Robb Ellis*

I have never seen a modern town comparable to New York. The color of the stone and the lightness of the air would put vitality into a corpse.

—*Margot Asquith*

I saw the skyscrapers in the deepening darkness become slowly
honeycombed with lights until, before I reached the Manhattan end,
these buildings piled up in a dazzling mass against the indigo sky.

—*Lewis Mumford*

I knew well those in the old furnished rooms up around Columbia.
They had about them a left-over, dim, vanquished aspect, depressed
spirits in a conquered territory.

—*Elizabeth Hardwick*

To be on the water in the dark and the wonder of electricity—[one
sees the] the real beauty of Manhattan.

—*James Schuyler*

When you give up your apartment in New York and move to another city, New York becomes the worst version of itself.

*—Nora Ephron on moving out of New York City and seeing all the negative aspects that New Yorkers miss or ignore while living there*

The water was glassy calm...shimmering with the light of a full moon . . . that made the hushed harbor seem like a collective dream of the sleeping city.

*—Michael Daly*

Beauty indeed was the aim of the creator of the spire of Trinity Church, so cruelly overtopped . . .

*—Henry James on how the rise of skyscrapers in Lower Manhattan dwarfed the beauty of Trinity Church*

The Hudson was a black ribbon beneath the cragged Jersey shore.

—*Mario Puzo*

Abandon your homes—we must build a bridge.

—*Robert Moses warning Brooklyn residents as he was about to start construction on the world's longest expansion bridge, the Verranzano Narrows, in 1964*

The city glides, like cities seen from the air, Mere smoke and sparkle to the passenger. . . . Having in mind another destination.

—*James Merrill*

The New York rivers dangled lights along the banks like lanterns on a wire.

—*Zelda Fitzgerald*

The skyscrapers looked like tall gravestones. I wondered why, if the United States was so rich, as surely it was, did its biggest city look so grotesque?

—*Bernardo Vega*

Greenwich Village—lovely, liberal Greenwich Village of the charming streets and historic brownstones—is poised on the edge of disaster.

—*Clark Whelton on the rise in crime in New York during the tumult of the late 1960s*

Not only was the Empire State Building built in an astonishing
thirteen months, but it was done almost entirely without overtime.

*—Thomas Kelly*

The Empire State Building is the lighthouse of Manhattan.

*—Robert A. M. Stern*

. . . everything I saw across the water added to New York's
sepulchral mystery.

*—Emily Barton*

They walk in silence for a block . . . the brightest lights of Times
Square, mesmerizing, each neon shape bleeding into the fog and
creating its own aura of color.

—*Kathryn Harrison*

Those skyscrapers, who belong to a brotherhood of giants, help
each other to rise, to prop each other up, to soar until all sense of
perspective disappears.

—*Paul Moran*

Welcome to the Twilight Zone—a block trapped in a dimension
between the city that is, and one that will never be again.

—*Steve Cuozzo on the block of West 36th
between 8th and 9th Avenues*

In ancient New York, everyone shared walls because it was cheap. If you can't take down shared walls you can't do development in New York.

—*Lawyer Mark Berman*

As a kid growing up in New York, the Empire State Building was the fixed point at the center of the earth.

—*Rick Bell*

More films now use New York as a backdrop, but it is too perky to have any character.

—*John Clay*

If each neighborhood were a nation, Lincoln Square might win points for patriotism.

—*C. J. Hughes*

The Dakota remains Mount Olympus in the mythology of New York apartment houses.

—*Christopher Gray*

I am the enchanted Orchard. My pyramids of stone and crystals rise rise rise.

—*Denise Lauture*

O West Side street that I am—I dip my toes in the hot sun—head
wreathed with the trees of Central Park.

—*D. H. Melhem*

Tremulously I stand in the subways, absorbed into the terrible
reverberations of exploding energy.

—*Helen Keller*

One thing you notice, as you approach New York City, is that
there are almost no signs saying "Manhattan." Instead the traveler
is introduced to such notions as "Mosholu" and "Major Deegan."

—*Nick Paumgarten*

23rd Street runs into heaven.

—*Max Blagg*

Like many natural beauties, New York is effortlessly photogenic.

—*Holland Cotter*

But, ah! Manhattan's sights and sounds, her smells, Her crowds, her throbbing force . . .

—*James Weldon Johnson*

I signed the lease because I wasn't ready to get a divorce from my building.

—*Nora Ephron*

Beyond the reflection the awning on Park Avenue stood like the guard at Buckingham Palace.

—*Anne Roiphe*

When engineers dream, they dream of bridges. Today, at its opening, the George Washington Bridge fulfills the dream of three generations.

—*L. B. Deyo on the 1932 opening of the bridge*

The George Washington Bridge over the Hudson is the most beautiful bridge in the world. Made of cables and steel beams, it gleams in the sky like a reversed arch. It is blessed. It is the only seat of grace in the disordered city.

—*Le Corbusier*

What can ever be more stately and admirable to me than mast-hemm'd Manhattan?

—*Walt Whitman*

Graffiti just looked and smelled a lot like being a rock star. If you did it good enough...everyone in the city would know your name.

—*Joseph Anatasio*

"*Mica schist*," he thought. "Manhattan *mica schist*. Ah, the pristine, naked, sparkling purity of it, come to light after aeons, as if awakening."

—*Henry Roth on the bedrock of Manhattan*

From the thundering underground—the maze of the New York subways—the world pours into Times Square. Like lost souls emerging from the purgatory of the trains . . .

*—John Rechy*

. . . in 1942, a man named Lou Walters opened a nightclub called the Latin Quarter, on the corner of Broadway and Forty-Eighth Street, the kind of place that no longer exists, except, in a way that doesn't count, in Las Vegas.

*—Nick Paumgarten*

I can never put on paper the thrill of the underground ride to Harlem. . . . At every station I kept watching for the sign: 135TH STREET. When I saw it, I held my breath.

*—Langston Hughes*

Her shining towers, her avenues, her slums—O God! the stark,
unutterable pity, To be dead, and never again behold my city!

—*James Weldon Johnson*

New York was more full of reflection than of itself—the only
concrete things in town were the abstractions.

—*Zelda Fitzgerald*

Under the streets are men who balance despair and exaltation.

—*Dante Rosita*

The City of New York: embattled, gallant, enduring . . .
—*D. H. Melhem*

~

The Park Avenue of poodles and polished brass; it is cab-country, tip town, glassville, a window-washer's paradise.
—*Gay Talese on the richest part of Park Avenue*

~

[New York] has fabulous bones and hardly any bad angles.
—*Holland Cotter*

~

As usual in New York, everything is torn down before you have time to care for it.

—*James Merrill*

In the shadow of the great stone abutments the old Knickerbocker houses linger like ghosts of a departed day.

—*Jacob Riis*

With the advent of night a fantastic city all of fire suddenly rises from the ocean into the sky.

—*Maxim Gorky*

Before New Yorkers burned or buried their waste, they pitched garbage out their windows onto city streets, where it was consumed by scavenging pigs and dogs.

—*Elizabeth Royte*

It was twilight when they drove down lower Fifth Avenue into the Square, and through the Arch behind them were the two long rows of pale violet lights that used to bloom so beautifully against the grey stone and asphalt.

—*Willa Cather*

On Park Avenue, above the Grand Central, many people—at a very high cost—believe they are living in style.

—*Edmund Wilson*

Eastward New York's luminosity lies in layers like a masonry of light and darkness built from the rocks to the night-sky.

—*Stephen Graham*

Brooklyn Bridge, the most superb piece of construction in the modern world . . . with strings of lights crossing it like glowing worms . . .

—*Hart Crane*

Who can deny that the Queensborough Bridge is the work of a creative artist?

—*Helen Keller*

I arrive in Times Square about six o' clock. It is Broadway's finest
hour. Here, until midnight, New York takes its bath of light.

—*Paul Morand*

"The Great White Way"—"The Roaring Forties"—all America
dreams of having a Broadway.

—*Paul Morand*

You hear little about West End Avenue. It is too genteel to have
much taste for publicity.

—*Christopher Morley*

From the ruins [of the old Waldorf Astoria], lonely and inexplicable as the sphinx, rose the Empire State Building.

*—F. Scott Fitzgerald*

Manhattan has been compelled to expand skyward because of the absence of any other direction in which to grow.

*—E. B. White*

But it was the Brooklyn Bridge that I loved best, its somber perfection of form, its cables stretched like a bowstring to shoot a steel arrow into our own age.

*—Lewis Mumford*

At the entrance to the Brooklyn Bridge, a new bank clerk pleads with the policeman to let him pass . . . although at that moment only death can cross the bridge.

> —*Jose Marti on the panic caused by the March* 1888 *snowstorm that shut New York down for almost a week*

The sunset lit up the sky, splashing the drab tenements with gold, bringing memories of Sabbath candles and the smell of gefilte fish.

> —*Anzia Yezierska*

. . . and coming out of the brownstone house
to the gray sidewalk, the watered street,
one side of the buildings rises with the sun
like a glistening field of wheat . . .

> —*Elizabeth Bishop*

The Barrio is shot. All the landmarks are gone. Nothin' but lousy projects with a piss-in self-service elevator.

—*Edwin Torres*

I could take the Harlem night and wrap it around you, take the neon lights and make you a crown.

—*Langston Hughes*

# II

# LOVE
## AND THE
# CITY

I am alone here in New York, no longer a we.
—*Elizabeth Hardwick on the loneliness
of being single in New York City*

The city breathes eroticism, from noon on. Even in the subway you can sense men and women angling, sizing each other up.
—*Garrison Keillor*

In the morning, they found his tap shoes on the Brooklyn Bridge, his wallet and wedding band inside them. All I remember is, it was the day before he turned forty.

—*Xu Xi*

New York is so crowded that sex turns into a spectator sport.

—*David McGlynn*

Commitment is a mystery here.

—*Candace Bushnell*

I dress for women—and I undress for men.

—*Angie Dickinson*

We were under a streetlight on the corner of West 50th Street and Tenth Avenue. The night and the streets were ours and the future lay sparkling ahead. And we thought we would know each other forever.

—*Lorenzo Carcaterra*

Nothing heals me of a sore and angry heart like a walk through the city I often feel denying me.

—*Vivian Gornick*

Morning comes to this city vacant of you. Pages and windows flare, and you are not there.

—*Li-Young Lee*

As though there were any suitable extra men in New York. . . . They're all queer. Or ought to be.

—*Truman Capote*

But how well did anybody really know anyone else in New York?

—*Candace Bushnell*

A New York divorce is in itself a diploma of virtue.

*—Edith Wharton*

In New York, I learned to make friends. Before, I never had any
friends, only conquests. I didn't have the time to find real friends.
I was being looked at, had no chance to look.

*—Marilyn Monroe*

In New York when a woman hits late middle age she becomes
invisible to men. They don't even see you.

*—Karen Fitzgerald*

I've seen sailors doing lots of things I couldn't dare paint. On Riverside Drive especially. It's always impressed me as a—well, very sordid place.

—*Paul Cadmus*

For my sins I live in the city of New York where love can stay only a minute.

—*Ted Berrigan*

In Harlem I found courage and joy and tolerance. I can be myself there. . . . They know all about me and I don't have to lie.

—*Blair Niles on being young and gay in Harlem and the acceptance he felt*

She was born the year I finished college, which in my beloved
Manhattan meant we were an entirely plausible couple.

—*Howell Raines*

A fast word about oral contraception. I asked a girl to go to bed with
me, she said, "No."

—*Woody Allen*

In New York it's better to be an old man's sweetheart than a young
man's slave . . .

—*Karen Fitzgerald*

Being gay in New York has been the best of times and the worst of times. But it's been a blast and I wouldn't give it up for anything.

—*Rich Buyer*

I liked to walk up Fifth Avenue and pick out romantic women from the crowd and imagine that in a few minutes I was going to enter their lives, and no one would ever know or disapprove.

—*F. Scott Fitzgerald*

Being single, as a woman in Manhattan, is the equivalent of having some dread social disease.

—*Tama Janowitz*

New York City . . . where even the ugly women are pretty.

—*David McGlynn*

New York is the great place for young adventurers. You can roam around, see incredibly weird things, be glamorous in ways impossible back home, and have sex with anybody you like and be secret about it.

—*Garrison Keillor*

New York is tough on lonely people.

—*Michael Bergin*

The woman looked glamorous to me here on Eighth Avenue at ten in the morning—richly haggard, a jewel in its natural setting.

—*Vivian Gornick*

I was lusted after walking down the streets of New York.

—*Janice Dickinson, the self-proclaimed supermodel, on being stared at by the horny men of New York*

There seems to be a pack of wooden-headed louts about this town, who fall in love with every old strumpet who smiles a flabby smile at them in a street car.

—*Mark Twain*

It is a New York loneliness, hot with shame, loneliness that tells you you're a fool and a loser.

—*Vivian Gornick*

If Paris is the setting for a romance, New York is the perfect city in which to get over one, to get over anything . . .

—*Cyril Connolly*

I can't wait until tomorrow . . . because I get better looking every day.

—*New York Jet Joe Namath*

Manhattan, that mecca of singles, has become less purposefully fascinating, now that the hunt is over.

—*Phillip Lopate*

New York friendship is an education in the struggle between devotion to the melancholy and attraction to the expressive.

—*Vivian Gornick*

With no subways running, budding romances have been nipped simply because she lives on the East Side and he lives on the West.

—*Nora Ephron*

New York was no mere city. It was instead an infinitely
romantic notion.

—*Joan Didion*

There is no friend, lover, or relative I want to be with as much as I
want to swing though the streets being jostled and bumped, catching
the eye of the stranger, feeling the stranger's touch.

—*Vivian Gornick*

. . . the real thing in New York, as it says in the song, [is] a Sunday
kind of love.

—*Tom Wolfe*

The solitary are obsessed. Apartments furnish little solitude.
—*George Oppen*

I associate energy, dark violence, sex and glamour with New York.
—*Catherine Schmitz*

Nobody gives a damn who you sleep with. In this world, it's who you're seen dining with that counts.
—*Maury "Cholly Knickerbocker" Paul*

That's all the Village is, honey, just one crazy little soap opera
after another . . .

—*Ann Bannon*

With the man I love who loves me not
I walked in the street-lamp flare
But oh, the girls who can ask for love
In the lights of Union Square.

—*Sara Teasdale*

My ex-wife said she was violated on the Upper West Side. I
was asked to comment and I said knowing her it wasn't a moving
violation.

—*Woody Allen*

[The Statue of Liberty] was my second symbol of New York.
The ferry boat stood for triumph, the girl for romance.

—*F. Scott Fitzgerald*

I liked all of it, being twenty-nine years old and in Manhattan in the
fall and drinking good champagne on Park Avenue.

—*Joe McGinniss*

# III

# THE TIMES
*AND*
## SEASONS
*OF*
# NEW YORK

Only in New York can an early summer drizzle seem so unrepentantly sullen.

—*Stephen King*

. . . sunshine would bite through the frosty urban wilderness to share a little warmth with the residents of Harlem, like the pope giving absolution to a group of jailhouse sinners.

—*Teddy Hayes*

Day after day in gray and desperate weather even, one can see its mystic aspiration above the skyscrapers of New York.

—*Paul Rosenfeld on the sky in New York*

Even the crisp, translucent New York twilight, hovering high
above the city, seems here to drift along in order to conceal the
missing afternoon.

—*Zelda Fitzgerald*

. . . in the warm months three to five cats a week fall from the city's
highrises. . . . But only a few die.

—*Howell Raines*

Before him, then, the slope stretched up and, above it the brilliant
sky, and beyond it, cloudy and far away he saw the skyscrapers on
New York.

—*James Baldwin*

Twilights were wonderful. . . . They hung above New York like an indigo wash . . .

—*Zelda Fitzgerald*

There is nothing more beautiful than New York City in the snow.
—*Mayor Rudy Giuliani*

one winter afternoon (at the magical hour when is becomes if) a bespangled clown standing on eighth street handed me a flower.

—*e.e.cummings*

The rain sees last options, called bluffs, final scenes, silenced bells, snuffed candles, books abruptly closed. At Broadway and 110th, the windshield wipers screech as they toss it from the glass.

—*Thomas H. Cook*

In the summer in New York, the streets turn into rivers of molten tar, like a Venice from hell, with crazed cabdrivers careening like possessed gondoliers.

—*David McGlynn*

It is five A.M. Something of the burden of the city has been lifted. The air is light. The heart seems freed.

—*Stephen Graham*

But I landed in New York to find the weather itself conspiring against me.

—*Ruth Reichel*

Night fell over the arctic waste of New York, and terror took over.

—*Jose Marti on the Blizzard of 1888*

New York lay in blue twilight as in a valley which the sun never comes to bake with heat.

—*Paul Rosenfeld*

It was a queer, sultry summer, the summer they electrocuted the Rosenbergs, and I didn't know what I was doing in New York.

*—Sylvia Plath*

. . . the sinister misery of the black, hot city night left me frozen in horror.

*—Dawn Powell*

. . . New York, at the beginning of March, is a hoyden we would not care to miss—a drafty wench, her temperature up and down, full of bold promises and dust in the eye.

*—E. B. White*

I myself like the climate of New York. . . . I see it in the air up between the street. . . . But the climate you don't use stays fresh and neat.

—*Edwin Denby*

Oh, do you feel the breeze from the subway? Isn't it delicious?
—*Marilyn Monroe in the film "The Seven Year Itch"*

. . . for in New York the advance of the seasons is not forgotten but intensified.

—*John Cheever*

Dawn in New York has four columns of mire and a hurricane of black pigeons splashing putrid waters.

—*Federico Garcia Lorca*

Now is the summer of our discothèques. And every night is a
party night.

—*Anthony Haden-Guest*

New York lay stretched in midsummer languor under her trees in her
thinnest dress, idly and beautifully to the eyes of her lover.

—*E. B. White*

. . . in a graying evening haze, humbly set foot on the Brooklyn
Bridge, as a conqueror presses into a city all shattered . . .

—*Vladimir Mayakovsky*

It was one of those late May evenings when New York seems to both hug you and summon you on towards some reward to be found in that city and nowhere else.

—*Howell Raines*

The night was oppressive . . . one of those New York summer evenings when even the walls seemed to sweat . . .

—*David Margolick*

For two days the snow has had New York in its power, encircled, terrified, like a prize fighter driven to the canvas by a sneak punch.

—*Jose Marti*

The day was hot and bright, and all New York seemed anxious to get away.

—*Theodore Dreiser*

At twilight on a foggy evening . . . it is beyond description. Gradually the lights in the enormously tall buildings begin to flicker through the mist . . .

—*Hart Crane*

. . . New York, heavy and stifling till night, has forgotten its hardships and height . . .

—*Vladimir Mayakovsky*

New York has a special interest for me when it is wrapped in a fog.
Then it behaves very much like a blind person.

—*Helen Keller*

The seamy side of Battery Park is the poor castaway who has sought
its coolness after a hot day of panhandling . . .

—*James Huneker*

On Forty-Second Street it is a glowing summer afternoon all night:
one might almost wear white trousers and straw hat.

—*Paul Morand*

# IV

# I LOVE
# NEW YORK

I've fallen in love with many cities, but only an orgasm lasting an hour could surpass the bliss of my first year in New York.

*—Truman Capote*

Every true New Yorker believes with all his heart that when a New Yorker is tired of New York, he is tired of life.

*—Robert Moses*

New York, hear this: Everything you have, Chicago has, too, but better.

*—Edward Kane*

I'd rather be a lamppost in New York than the mayor of Chicago.

*—NYC Mayor Jimmy Walker*

I fled New England and came to Manhattan, that island off the coast of America, where human nature was king and everyone exuded character and had a big attitude.

—*Spalding Gray*

The city held, I thought, every adventure I hadn't imagined . . . a place to reincarnate, or pull a whole new existence from the chatter of crowded streets.

—*Carole Radziwill, "What Remains"*

Already I was possessed of the New York disease: a fervish desire to appear knowing, no matter how deep one's ignorance.

—*Mary Cantwell*

Out in my garden the sun is shining, the flowers are preening, a bunch of blue jays are gangsta rapping. And I'm sitting here yearning for all of you in Manhattan, all smoking and drinking and shopping and cursing, all totally unaware of the spiritual revolution taking place west of the Hudson.

—*Cynthia Heimel*

Today he was going to Harlem. The home of the funkiest brothas in the world.

—*Teddy Hayes*

The things that go wrong are what make this the second toughest job in America. But the things that go right are those things that make me want it.

—*New York's Mayor John V. Lindsay in 1969*

New York is still here. We've suffered terrible losses and we will
grieve for them, but we will be here, tomorrow and forever.
                    —*Mayor Rudy Giuliani in a speech after the attack*
                *on the World Trade Center on September 11, 2001*

I've always loved New York. It just never loved me back.
                                —*James Edwards, a homeless man*

. . . I still did not lose that sense of wonder about New York. I began
to cherish the loneliness of it, the sense that at any given time no one
need know where I was or what I was doing.
                                                —*Joan Didion*

. . . luckily, there's enough positive to keep us here, and the negative is what makes the positive more intense.

—*Tama Janowitz*

One of the things about leaving Hollywood and coming to New York and attending the Actor's Studio is that I feel I can afford to be more myself. After all, if I can't be myself who can I be? I would like to know.

—*Marilyn Monroe*

New York City—the place with the most gorgeous women and the best food in the world.

—*Bob Dylan*

The city's got the right name—New York. Nothing ever gets old around here.

—*Ralph Stephenson*

If I live in New York, it is because I choose to live here. It is the city of total intensity, the city of the moment.

—*Diana Vreeland*

God! The Restaurants! New York has become the Florence of the 16th Century. Genius on every corner.

—*John Guare*

Where is this Hollywood scene, where is it? I'd like to find it one day. . . . If I want to go out and have a good time, I go to New York.

—*Natasha Henstridge*

I miss New York. I still love how people talk to you on the street—just assault you and tell you what they think of your jacket.

—*Madonna*

I love New York City. Everyone is busy with their own lives—and no one is interested in some Hollywood celebrity walking past in downtown Manhattan.

—*James Van Der Beek*

And New York is the most beautiful city in the world? It is not far from it. No urban night is like the night there. . . . Squares after squares of flame. . . . Here is our poetry, for we have pulled down the stars to our will.

*—Ezra Pound*

I bought a burrito at a Vietnamese-owned and staffed restaurant that advertises "Authentic & Fresh Tex-Mex." I stood on a subway platform and watched a band of ethnic Japanese-Peruvians play a Spanish-titled pop song using Greek instruments. This is my New York. I think if I lived in Middle America, I'd feel like I was from another planet.

*—Joe Jervis*

. . . little has changed in our New York neighborhoods except the faces, the names, and the languages spoken. The same decent values of hard work and accomplishment and service to city and nation still exist.

*—Mayor David Dinkins*

I've been partying pretty hard. They should really consider renaming New York Binge City. It destroys me, but I have fun.

*—Gina Gershon*

New York is the perfect place to be a hermit. You can have everything delivered.

*—Cynthia Ceilan*

Some day this old Broadway shall climb to the skies,
as a ribbon of cloud on a south wind shall rise.

*—Nicholas Vachel Lindsay*

At Broadway, shining Broadway
only my heart, my heart is lonely . . .

*—Claude McKay*

Yep, I hear the music already. Like a trumpet solo mufflin' a long
note, far away . . . sounds like Miles. Maybe that's where people go
when they die . . . Birdland.

*—Edwin Torres*

The fellow in the bar was playing "Autumn in New York." From this distance, it had an echoey sound, like music heard in a dream.

—*Stephen King*

New York City
the melting pot
Gets sucked in through tight lips
Turns to smoke and ash
and gets you high.

—*Steve Geary*

For one brief golden moment rare like wine,
The gracious city swept across the line . . .

—*Claude McKay*

I hear the halting footsteps of a lass
In Negro Harlem when the night lets fall
Its veil. I see shapes of girls who pass . . .

—*Claude McKay*

How funny you are today in New York
like Ginger Rogers in Swingtime . . .

—*Frank O'Hara*

She dreamed, lulled by the train, of getting off at heaven or
New York City, whichever she got to first.

—*Mary Lee Settle*

I can't wait to get back to New York City where at least when I walk down the street, no one hesitates to tell me exactly what they think of me.

—*Ani DiFranco*

I go to Paris, I go to London, I go to Rome, and I always say, "There's no place like New York." It's the most exciting city in the world now.

—*Robert DeNiro*

There was always a love-hate relationship with New York and the rest of America, but I made them feel more love than hate.

—*Mayor Ed Koch*

A hundred times have I thought New York is a catastrophe, and fifty times it is a beautiful catastrophe.

—*Le Corbusier*

I love New York City. I've got a gun.

—*Charles Barkley, former NBA superstar*

New York! I've always wanted to see it and now I've seen it. It's true what they say—it's the most wonderful city in the world.

—*Betty Smith*

I was born in New York; somewhere between heaven and hell.

—*Ernie Koy*

[On September 11] the Fire Department of New York was savagely wounded, and its collective heart was brutally broken.

—*Russell Feliciano*

I wandered around my native city in a daze, trying to think of ways I could protect New York from future terrorist attacks.

—*Erica Jong*

The West Side streets of Manhattan were our private playground,
a cement kingdom where we felt ourselves to be nothing less than
absolute rulers.

*—Lorenzo Carcaterra*

I love New York because within its borders you can travel the world.

*—Dennis Gonzalez*

New York, thy name is irreverence and hyperbole. And grandeur.

*—Ada Louise Huxtable*

This city is the center of the universe.

—*Mayor Robert F. Wagner*

The very idea of being in New York was dreamlike, for like
many young Negroes of the time, I thought of it as the freest of
American cities and considered Harlem as the site and symbol
of Afro-American progress and hope.

—*Ralph Ellison*

Here was my city, immense, overpowering, flooded with energy
and light.

—*Lewis Mumford*

If you look at pigeons, they are quite beautiful. Imagine a city
without them rising into the sky.

*—Lucy Kuemmerle*

He took long walks to recapture the old New York that was dying
with him.

*—Louis Auchincloss*

The general look of painting today strikes me as seductive. It makes
the miles of New York galleries as luxurious to wander through as a
slave market.

*—Edwin Denby*

New York is like heroin to the soul.

*—Nina Kurtz*

Manhattan Island, at its center, inspires utterly baseless optimism—
even in me, even in drunks sleeping in a doorway . . .

*—Kurt Vonnegut*

In some ways New York affects me like Venice. It's in danger of
dying, so there's something tender about it.

*—Filmmaker Paul Mazursky*

That's what I love about the NYPD. . . . It's more than a job—it's a
front row ticket to the best show on Earth.

*—NYPD Det. Ken Robinson*

Better a square foot of New York than all the rest of the world in a lump.

*—Texas Guinan*

Other cities consume culture, New York creates it.

*—Paul Goldberger*

The experience of visiting New York City for me, a born and bred Southerner, has been similar to sending electric charges through my body . . . it's been pleasurable.

*—David Crowe*

The streets never failed them. It was an immense excitement. It never slept. It roared like a sea. It exploded like fireworks.
*—Michael Gold on the explosiveness*
*of the New York City streets*

Small, inexpensive restaurants are the home fires of New York City.
*—Maeve Brennan*

And this is my first chicken since the night I left New York and the waiter asked me if to keep the menu as a memory . . .
*—J. P. Donleavy*

I was in love with Harlem long before I got there.
*—Langston Hughes*

To me, a Westchester teenager, New York offered an irresistible cocktail of fear and grandeur. It lured as much by its dangers and squalor as by its riches.

*—L. B. Deyo*

Manhattan. . . . How fit a name for America's great democratic island city!

*—Walt Whitman*

Cherish this city
left you by default
include it in your daydreams.

*—Audre Lorde*

. . . as I pass, O Manhattan, your frequent and swift flash of eyes offering me love . . .

—*Walt Whitman*

That is one of the things I loved best about Brooklyn. Everyone is not expected to be exactly like everyone else.

—*Carson McCullers*

I went up the steps and out into the bright September sunlight. Harlem! I stood there, dropped my bags, took a deep breath and felt happy again.

—*Langston Hughes*

My New York City talks to me all the time, whispers in my ear, keeps me grounded, thrills me . . . is my constant lover.

—*Annette Myers*

There again was my lost city, wrapped cool in mystery and promise.

—*F. Scott Fitzgerald*

New York is full of moments. . . . It is performance art. It is the great leveler.

—*Annette Myers*

New York is just too big, too complex to be served by any one writer. At best he can only offer his little tribute to something he loves, but which is beyond him.

—*Robert Moses*

And our memories
hit the windowpane
finding heaven
in a sewer.

—*Amy Ahuja*

# V

# FEAR
## *AND*
# LOATHING
## *IN*
# NEW YORK

More than 150 heads of state attended the UN Summit, giving
New Yorkers a chance to get in touch with prejudices they didn't
even know they had.

—*Jon Stewart*


It is an art form to hate New York City properly.

—*Pat Conroy*


. . . we were heading through the Lincoln Tunnel which seemed
longer and fumier than ever, like Hell, with tiled walls.

—*Philip Roth*

I was always crazy about New York, dependent on it, scared of it—
well, it is dangerous—but beyond that there was the pressure of
being young and of not yet having done work you really liked,
trademark work, breakthrough work.

—*Harold Brodsky*

In Manhattan if your ass was on fire, they wouldn't piss on it to put
it out.

—*Joe Flaherty*

. . . this was New York City, where nutcases not only walked the
streets freely but were elected to high office, hosted programs on TV,
and ran the biggest and best institutions.

—*Teddy Hayes*

. . . they passed through a tunnel and arrived in New York City.
It smelled of urine back then: It wasn't safe.

*—Candace Bushnell*

New York is too strenuous for me; it gets on my nerves.

*—Ambrose Bierce*

New York was, of course, intolerable. I found that I was organizing
my day around those times when it was possible—just possible—to
get a cup of coffee without standing in a line a half hour.

*—David Mamet*

New York is appalling, fantastically charmless, and elaborately dire.
—*Henry James*

~

New York City has become a metaphor for what looks like the last days of American civilization . . . it's run by fools. Its citizens are at the mercy of its criminals. . . . The air is foul. The traffic is impossible. Services are diminishing and the morale is such that ordering a cup of coffee in a diner can turn into a request for a fat lip.
—*New York Times film critic Vincent Canby,*
*November 10, 1974*

~

I entered New York hospital with trepidation. His private room was full of flowers and death was in the air.
—*Claude Saks*

~

New York has all that intense hatred and pain—just torture—where everything is ten times as hard as it needs to be, and everything is terribly important.

—*Beth Anderson*

New York is something awful, something monstrous. I like to walk the streets, lost, but I recognize that New York is the world's greatest lie. New York is Senegal with machines.

—*Federico Garcia Lorca*

As the mystique of Harlem grew, white people became increasingly curious.

—*Linda Tarrant-Reid*

New York floats in the universal mind, to some a glittering symbol, to others a tempting target.

—*Rich Lamb*

New York was panicking, terrified. . . . There were literally hundreds of thousands of people sick simultaneously . . . the death toll ultimately reached thirty-three thousand for New York alone.

—*John M. Barry on the 1918 Spanish Flu epidemic*

The Devil lives in New York. I've seen him. Here he walks the streets.

—*David Davis*

I was able to tear the veil of racism in New York.
>—*Al Sharpton after residents of Bensonhurst, Brooklyn, were shown on TV throwing watermelons at blacks and flinging racial insults*

If Broadway is a "state of mind," as some phrase inventor put it, a clinical psychologist should diagnose it. He might isolate the precise form of dementia that drives this wacky world.
>—*Jack Lait and Lee Mortimer*

New York throbs with impatience and aggression, suspicion and paranoia just below the surface, the hysteria and panic always latent.
>—*Bob Brody*

Living in New York in this really weird time. . . . People are
constantly waiting for something bad to happen.
                           —*Sam Endicott after September 11, 2001*

New York is a crime-ridden city. . . . Immorality is rampant.
                           —*Reverend Billy Graham*

This is New York, and I am a stranger in a nightmare . . .
                           —*Carl Van Doren*

Every now and then, seeking to rid my mind of thoughts of death
and doom, I get up early and go down to the Fulton Fish Market.
                           —*Joseph Mitchell*

O hopeless city of idiots, empty-eyed, staring, afraid, red beam top'd car at street curb arrived.

—*Allen Ginsberg*

New York City is a tough hard place and it does not need a mean-spirited mayor like Giuliani. He is a little man looking for a balcony to speak from.

—*Jimmy Breslin*

In New York it seems really true that only the good die young.

—*Justin Alomar*

. . . the idea of decay is nothing new to New York.

—*Vincent J. Cannato*

I have often thought that it would begin in New York. This
metropolis has all the symptoms of a mind gone berserk.

—*Isaac Bashevis Singer on where a
revolution might start in America*

I carry more cash than I should and walk the street at night without
feeling scared, unless someone scary passes.

—*James Schuyler*

All of a sudden it was great out there on the street in New York. All
those damnable millions who come careening into Manhattan all
week weren't there. The town was empty.

—*Tom Wolfe on the joys of a Sunday
morning in New York City*

In Russia people suffered, but I have never met as many maniacs there as in New York City.

—*Isaac Bashevis Singer*

Mayor Bloomberg's more Mary Poppins than Dirty Harry.

—*Billy Gorta*

Life in New York was spooky and odd, especially to a hormonal pre-teen.

—*Catherine Schmitz*

Where are the service workers supposed to live, in rat holes? This [city] is becoming a class system.

—*Jerry Scott Alexander McCoy*

New York City is simply too big. I have lived in it for too long to
hate it, but I know it too well to love it.

> —*Former New York firefighter and*
> *current author Dennis Smith*

This wasn't Park Avenue. This was the jungle. You could bet your ass
there was going to be gunfire tonight.

> —*NYPD Officer Wilton Seker on July 13, 1977, in*
> *Bushwick, Brooklyn, as New York had a blackout*

By the mid-1970s Bushwick was . . . a prison of traumatized welfare
recipients reeling in rage and despair.

> —*Jim Sheeper*

There are eight million naked cities in this naked city—they dispute
and disagree.

—*Colson Whitehead*

On September 11, 2001, he opened his eyes at 4 A.M. . . .
and Muhammad Atta's last day began. And that name, the
name he journeyed under, itself like a promise of vengeance:
Muhammad Atta.

   —*Martin Amis on the leader of the 9/11 hijackers that flew two*
     *planes into the World Trade Center and one into the Pentagon*

Crazed with avarice, lust and rum . . . New York, thy
name's Delirium.

—*B.R.Newton*

In the tenements life was close; a young woman without a man
was dangerous. She could draw off money and goods as the leech
draws blood . . .

—*Mario Puzo*

. . . there's not much Rudy Giuliani did wrong on 9/11. That's because
there wasn't much to do. Events controlled the response, not the
other way around.

—*Billy Gorta*

When you made a mistake at the *New York Times*, you were held up to
public ridicule.

—*Ruth Reichel on the* New York Times' *claim*
*to being the gold standard of newspapers*

A writer in New York is a little bit like a tree falling in a forest. You're never sure if somebody's going to hear you.

—*Lucinda Franks*

We ought to change the sign on the Statue of Liberty to read, "This time around, send us your rich."

—*Felix Rosalyn*

The city had beaten the pants off me. Whatever it required to get ahead, I didn't have it. I didn't leave the city in disgust—I left it with the respect plain unadulterated fear gives.

—*John Steinbeck*

To white people, even Ed Bradley and Bryant Gumble waiting to cross the street is potentially scary.

*—Chris Rock, Brooklyn-raised comedian*

We don't have [Martin Luther] King's vision of America today. We have hypocrites saying the devils are in Selma, Alabama, but they are in New York, too.

*—Gay Talese*

You talk about racism in Alabama but you have racism here in New York, too. I don't see any black people down there in Central Park.

*—Gov. George Wallace on a 1966 visit to New York City, looking out his window from his Central Park South hotel*

[New York is] the least loved city of any great cities. . . . Why should it be loved as a city? It is never the same city for a dozen years altogether.

—Harper's Magazine, *1856*

You know the difference between a New York City bartender and a proctologist? A proctologist only has to deal with one asshole at a time.

—*Chris Santangelo*

. . . Protect them from harm in the performance of their duties to stop crime, robberies, riots, and violence.

—*A policeman's prayer displayed in the lobby of Brooklyn's 60th precinct*

And the grand finale? A fistfight, after which somebody gets
run over. Listen, if I want to see that kind of action, I don't go to
Shanghai. I don't even go to the movies. I go to the South Bronx
and stand outside a bar.

—*Anthony Lane, reviewing* Mission Impossible III,
*in* The New Yorker

You cannot live in New York . . . and not be aware that vast tonnages
of waste are generated daily.

—*Elizabeth Royte*

This ain't my town. It's a town you come to for a short time.
It's murder.

—*Ernest Hemingway*

Despite attempts to be liberal-minded, I can't shake my retrograde prejudices about those who live in this urban hell. Images of knife-wielding maniacs and muttering schizophrenics dominate my mind.

—*David Liebowitz*

[Langston] Hughes posed the widely recognized question, "What happens to a dream deferred?" in response to the changes he had witnessed in Harlem.

—*Linda Tarrant-Reid on how Harlem descended into urban blight after all the hope Hughes had for the neighborhood in the 1930s*

. . . respectable people avoid the Bowery as far as possible at night. Every species of crime and vice is abroad at this time watching for its victims . . .

—*James D. McCabe*

. . . but you learn to keep your opinions to yourself on the Bowery if you don't want to run into trouble.

—*Jimmy Durante*

I just have claustrophobia in New York . . . I lose my feeling of identification there. It's too big . . . I feel tense in New York.

—*William Inge*

With nights of unabating bitterness; They cannot reach you in your safe retreat, the city's hate, the city's prejudice . . .

—*Claude McKay*

Lower Manhattan was soon a furnace of crimson flames, from which there was no escape.

*—H. G. Wells, 1907*

The goaded city gives, not day
Nor night can ease her heart,
her anguished labours stay . . .

*—Amy Lowell*

I always used to go to the Bronx Zoo. . . . I love to go to the zoo. But not on Sundays. I don't like to see the people making fun of the animals, when it should be the other way around.

*—Ernest Hemingway*

The subway is great, man, but I'll tell you if you were counting where all the insane people in New York are, they're riding the C train.

—*Matt Dillon*

In this motley, cosmopolitan city, a broth enriched by two worlds, true citizens are hard to find. The rabble, the plebian mass, dominates.

—*Ernest Duvergier de Hauranne*

When ladies go shopping in New York, they generally expect to enjoy themselves; though Heaven knows, they must be hard up for resources to fancy this mode of spending their time.

—*Fanny Fern*

Nine out of ten street beggars in New York are unworthy objects, and to give to them is simply to encourage vagrancy . . .

—*James D. McCabe*

A horde of dirty children play about the dripping hydrant, the only thing in the alley that thinks enough of its chance to make the most of it: it is the best it can do.

—*Jacob Riis*

But it is necessary to make money, and in the commodious corners of the bright city, as everywhere in the world, depravity laughs disdainfully at hypocrisy and falsehood.

—*Maxim Gorky*

The fashionable New Yorker, male or female, is powerless against the charms of aristocracy.

*—James D. McCabe*

One thing alone is good in the garish city: You can drink in hatred to your soul's content . . .

*—Maxim Gorky*

But every man, Jack, when he first sets foot on the stones of Manhattan has got to fight. . . . Your opponent is the City.

*—O. Henry*

There is no city in the Union in which imposters of all kinds flourish so well as in New York.

*—James D. McCabe*

With the very symbol of liberty, that stupid giant female, with her illuminating torch, becomes a monster of hated men, her torch a club that ominously threatens us: Get to work! Get to work!

—*James Huneker*

People I know in New York are incessantly on the point of going back where they came from to write a book . . .

—*A. J. Liebling*

. . . taking cabs in the middle of the night,
driving as if to save your soul
where the road goes round and round the park
and the meter glares like a moral owl . . .

—*Elizabeth Bishop*

I am still so amazed at the brazenness of people—completely New York people—who only remember you when you've gone into your fourth printing.

—*Dawn Powell*

Moving into a new block is a big jump for a Harlem kid. You're torn up from your hard-won turf and brought into an "I don't know you" block, where every kid is your enemy.

—*Piri Thomas*

A dreadful night voice praying to a leering city night god.

—*Dawn Powell*

The streets of Harlem make an unreal scene of frightened silence at 2 A.M. . . . Like everything got a lay-off from noise and hassling.

—*Piri Thomas*

The plain fact of the matter is that New York is too good for New Yorkers.

—*Heywood Broun*

# VI

# SPORTIN'
# NEW YORK

Wake up muscles. We're in New York now.

*—Casey Stengel*

New York is not a city to return to in defeat.

*—Moss Hart*

The faces in New York remind me of people who played a game and lost.

*—Murray Kempton*

I don't understand the press. They write about what you say, not what you do.

*—New York Yankee Thurman Munson*

A city struggling for survival can't lose a single hero.
>                     —*Newspaperman Pete Hamill on the New*
>                     *York Mets trade of Tom Seaver in 1977*

You take a team with twenty-five assholes and I'll show you a
pennant. I'll show you the New York Yankees.
>                                           —*Bill Lee*

Hating the Yankees is as American as pizza pie, unwed mothers, and
cheating on your income tax.
>                                           —*Mike Royko*

It was as if I had seen New York across a crowded room, caught her eye, but never got the chance to talk to her. Now I was talking to her, feeling her. Being seduced by her.

—*New York Yankee Reggie Jackson*

The starting line of the New York City Marathon is kind of a giant time bomb behind you about to go off. It is the most spectacular start in sports.

—*Bill Rodgers*

My kid was a great baseball player. I thought I had it made. Front row seats at Yankee Stadium. Then he turned sixteen and wanted to be a rapper.

—*James Caan*

I'd like to thank the good Lord for making me a Yankee.

—*Joe DiMaggio*

In New York now, they have the Harvey Milk High School for gay students. They don't have much of a football team, but the halftime show . . .

—*Bill Maher*

The biggest thing I don't like about New York are the foreigners. You can walk an entire block in Times Square and not hear anybody speaking English.

—*John Rocker, former Atlanta Braves pitcher*

God is living in New York and he's a Met fan.

—*Tom Seaver*

Sports is the toy department of life.

—*Howard Cosell*

New York's a tough town without the coin, isn't it? You never get a glance when you're out of the game.

—*Theodore Dreiser*

Some kids want to join the circus...others want to be big-league players. . . . When I came I came to the Yankees I got to do both.

—*New York Yankee Graig Nettles*

There is no room in baseball for discrimination. It is our national pastime and a game for all.

*—New York Yankee Lou Gehrig*

When we won the league championship . . . I had to thank all the single broads in New York.

*—New York Jet Joe Namath*

It gets late early out there.

*—New York Yankee Yogi Berra on playing baseball at Yankee Stadium in the fall*

New Yorkers love it when you spill your guts out there. Spill your guts at Wimbledon and they made you stop and clean it up.

—*Jimmy Connors*

Winning means everything! You show me a good loser and I'll show you a loser.

—*New York Yankee owner George Steinbrenner*

I was there when the flannel turned to double knit.

—*New York Met Tom Seaver*

Yells for the Mets were also yells for ourselves, a wry,
half-understood recognition that there is more Met than
Yankee in every one of us.

                                                *—Roger Angell*

I don't know how a businessman can walk into a community with
overcrowded schools and ask the city for a dime. That's what's
happening in New York. . . . The city's in this huge debt mode, and
they're going to spend hundreds of millions on a stadium?

                    *—Former New York Yankee Jim Bouton on
the building of a new Yankee Stadium*

Are they going to move to Charlotte? They're the New York
Yankees, making more money by far than any other club, and it's
in this market, in the Bronx. Where are they going to go?

                                                *—Neil Sullivan*

Pitching is the art of instilling fear.
            —*Sandy Koufax*

. . . no boy from a rich family ever made it to the big leagues.
            —*Joe DiMaggio*

Pro football is like nuclear warfare. There are no winners,
only survivors.
            —*Frank Gifford*

A team is where a boy can prove his courage on his own. A gang is
where a coward goes to hide.
            —*Mickey Mantle*

When you win, nothing hurts.

—*Joe Namath*

What I found when I came to New York was an atmosphere
of corruption. The only friend you have here is the money in
your pocket.

—*Former New York Met Victor Martinez*

I don't care who you are, you hear those boos.

—*New York Yankee Mickey Mantle*

I could never play in New York. The first time I came into a game
there, I got into the bullpen car and they told me to lock the doors.

—*Baltimore Oriole pitcher Mike Flanagan*

The rent here is really high, yo.

—*New York Met Derek Bell*

I didn't come to New York to be a star. I brought my own star with me.

—*New York Yankee Reggie Jackson*

I'm just more suited for the Mets. I find quixotic dignity in holding on, in waiting for it. They don't call them the Miracle Mets for nothing. Long-suffering makes miracles from the mundane.

—*Dave Hollander*

You say your friend stopped watching the Knicks. I say once a Knick always a Knick.

—*Willis Reed*

Heroes play in New York. Your career is not finished until you play in New York.

—*Dwight "Doc" Gooden*

Somehow for the Jets I feel Shea was their home. I mean, they were called the Jets for a reason. LaGuardia Airport is a stone's throw from the stadium . . . they are the New York Giants and the New York Jets. There's nothing New Jersey about these teams.

—*John Riggins*

Food runs.

—*New York Jet John Riggins on chasing down and tackling a mugger who ran away from him*

So I got shipped over to New York in a trade, which was the best thing that happened to me.

—*Lou Pinella*

What did I want when I was a kid in Brooklyn? I wanted the Dodgers to win the pennant.

—*"Grandpa" Al Lewis*

I like being an underdog in New York, because New Yorkers love an underdog.

—*Bob Guadio*

Even on a gorgeous afternoon in the midst of the best start that any Met fan could hope for, you knew the boos were coming.

*—John Harper*

Who is that girl in the dugout, with the long hair? What's going on here. . . . I won't say that women belong in the kitchen but they don't belong in the dugout.

*—New York Met broadcaster Keith Hernandez*

I was at Gleason's Gym in Brooklyn the other day, and boxing is still alive and well there, if only in memory.

*—Bill Gallo*

If there are baseball gods, the Yankees will be punished for this. The curse of Babe Ruth is going to come visiting them saying, "You've paved over my hallowed ground for a few bucks."
—*Former New York Yankee pitcher Jim Bouton on the tearing down of the old Yankee Stadium for a new stadium*

They're booing right now, but before I'm through everyone will be cheering.
—*New York Yankee Manager Billy Martin on the mercurial moods of New York sports fans*

I was a great walker and would walk from Ebbetts Field on Bedford Avenue straight down Eastern Parkway to Brownsville. You know what kind of a walk that is? But when the Dodgers won, it wasn't walking, it was flying.
—*"Grandpa" Al Lewis*

The Tom Seaver trade is much more than just a loss by the New York Mets . . . the trade is a serious loss to New York City.

—*Edward Edelson*

I was the DH, all right. Designated Hebrew.

—*Former New York Yankee Ron Blomberg*

I remember when I told my father I had bought the Yankees, he said to me: "You're better off sticking to ship building."

—*George Steinbrenner*

I'm George Foster. I love this team. The Mets are better than the Red Machine.

*—Former New York Met George Foster on a failed rap record he did in 1986 with other Mets*

The term Bronx Zoo fit . . . because we were a great soap opera.

*—Former New York Yankee Ron Guidry on the 1978 Yankees*

They give you cash, which is just as good as money.

*—Former New York Yankee Yogi Berra*

I don't think in his heart he was anything but a Yankee.
> *—Diana Munson on her late husband,*
> *New York Yankee Thurman Munson*

He was always hurting. He was a walking cast.
> *—Former New York Yankee Ron Guidry*
> *on teammate Thurman Munson*

In New York we simply assumed that we were the best—in baseball
as well as intellect, in brashness and in subtlety, in everything—and it
would have been unseemly to remark upon such an obvious fact.
> *—Michael Harrington*

It takes time to get adjusted to New York.

*—New York Mets owner Fred Wilpon*

Reggie Bush cried the last time he was in New York. He broke down and sobbed like a child when he won the Heisman Trophy . . .

*—Lenn Robbins*

Our goal is to put NASCAR on the front page of every New York City newspaper. New York is the place to be, everyone knows that.

*—Michael Printup*

Madison Square Garden to me and my mind is the Mecca of Maul.
New York is calling Yankee Stadium The Big Orchard . . .

*—Art Rust Jr.*

Everything is big time. There's an air and a snap and a tang to Manhattan that is generated by championship rather than mobilizations
of people and money.

*—Jack Lait and Lee Mortimer*

Pinstripe Pride ain't what it used to be.

*—Phil Mushnick on the hard times
facing the 2006 New York Yankees*

Ruth weighed 254, his pulse was high. He was as near to being a total loss as any patient I have ever had.

> —*Artie McGovern, trainer for New York Yankee Babe Ruth, who in 1925 is credited with saving Ruth's career with a new, strict diet and exercise regimen*

I better remember to acknowledge the guys in the bleachers the first time they chant my name.

> —*New York Yankee Johnny Damon on the bleacher roll call at Yankee Stadium*

Ranger fans have summarized everything that's wonderful about the most devoted of the New York faithful: we have long memories, we are unforgiving, we are unshakably loyal . . .

> —*Mike Vaccaro*

To be able to play in front of eight million Jews! Can't beat it. I lit everyone's candles for bar mitzvah in the city.

—*Former New York Yankee Ron Blomberg*

Looks Like Jesus. . . . Acts Like Judas

—*Tee shirts sold in Boston mocking*
*New York Yankee Johnny Damon*

Only a certain type of athlete can really thrive in New York.

—*Former New York Jet Coach Al Groh*

Slightly more than sixteen years apart, Steve Howe and Billy Martin, two troubled baseball souls whose notorious times occurred with the Yankees, died in similar accidents while riding in their pick-up trucks.

—*Murray Chass*

There are better places than Aqueduct on an ordinary Thursday afternoon, when only a handful of hardened gamblers are in the stands and the horses on the card are pedestrian types whose main function is to give people something to bet on.

—*Bill Finley*

Can't anybody here play this game?

—*New York Met manager Casey Stengel, as he watched the 1962 Mets—the worst team in baseball history with a record of 40 wins and 120 losses*

. . . she gave me a Mets sweatshirt, which I wear when I work, for luck . . .

—*Anne Roiphe*

. . . this guy . . . tells me that he and Babe Ruth were friends . . . there was never any doubt in his mind that Babe was Black. They drank together, played cards on 136th St. . . .

—*Art Rust Jr.*

I never heard a crowd boo a homer, but I've heard plenty of boos after a strikeout.

—*Babe Ruth*

And all around the town the fight mob talked about Lou Stillman and guys laughed. Laughter is a beautiful obituary.

*—Jimmy Cannon*

I've lost all respect for New York fans.

*—David Wells, former Yankee now Red Sox, after being heckled and booed by formerly adoring Yankee fans*

All I know . . . I pass people on the street and they don't know whether to say hello or goodbye.

*—New York Yankee manager Billy Martin, who was hired and fired five times by the Yankees*

I felt alone out there, like I was on a desert island. I felt like Gilligan.
—*New York Yankee centerfielder Mickey Rivers
on the vastness of Yankee Stadium*

To play eighteen years in Yankee Stadium is the best thing that could happen to a ballplayer.
—*Mickey Mantle*

Interesting. I learned they don't rebuild in New York.
—*Former New York Met manager Art Howe*

Even though they are considered the second team in New York, I believe the Mets reflect a more "New York State of Mind."
—*Art Rust Jr.*

If it wasn't for baseball, I'd be in either the penitentiary or the cemetery.

*—Babe Ruth*

New York is the place where everyone will stop a championship fight to look at an usher giving a drunk the bum's rush.

*—Damon Runyon*

I may not have been the best Yankee to put on pinstripes, but I am the proudest.

*—Billy Martin*

# VII

# FAMOUS
# NEW YORKERS

God is a concept by which we measure our pain.

—*John Lennon*

I've been on a calendar, but never on time.

—*Marilyn Monroe*

It's no fun being married to an electric light.

—*Joe DiMaggio, on his marriage to Marilyn Monroe*

A man is a god in ruins.

—*Duke Ellington*

Everything in life is luck.

—*Donald Trump*

Better to fail in originality than to succeed in imitiation.

—*Herman Melville*

My parents stayed together forty years, but that was out of spite.

—*Woody Allen*

Imagination is the highest kite one can fly.

—*Lauren Bacall*

I never lied to any man because I don't fear anyone. The only time you lie is when you are afraid.

—*John "The Dapper Don" Gotti*

Never open your mouth, unless you are in a dentist chair.

—*Sammy "The Bull" Gravano*

You can get much further with a kind word and a gun then you can with a kind word alone.

—*Al Capone*

Life is full of misery, loneliness, and suffering. And it is all over much too soon.

— *Woody Allen*

We moved closer to the sanitarium—less driving to do.
—*Art Carney on his repeated hospitalizations for alcoholism*

I feel your scorn and I accept it.

—*Jon Stewart*

Evolution can go to hell as far as I am concerned. What a mistake we are.

—*Kurt Vonnegut*

Electricity is really just organized lightning.

—*George Carlin*

All literature is gossip.

—*Truman Capote*

You only grow when you are alone.

—*Paul Newman*

Better sleep with a sober cannibal than a drunken Christian.

—*Herman Melville*

I am like a monk with a taste for hookers.

—*Moby*

Woman have been trained to speak softly and carry lipstick.
Those days are over.

—*Bella Abzug*

Eighty percent of success is showing up.

—*Woody Allen*

There are nights when the wolves are silent and only the
moon howls.

—*George Carlin*

We forget the little things, so it's no wonder some of us screw up the big things.

—*Neil Cavuto*

You show people what you're willing to fight for when you fight your friends.

—*Sen. Hillary Clinton*

A word to the wise ain't necessary —it's the stupid ones that need the advice.

—*Bill Cosby*

God isn't dead—he's just missing in action.

—*Phil Ochs*

The art of love is largely the art of persistence.

—*Albert Ellis*

Give a critic an inch and he'll write a book.

—*John Steinbeck*

If at first you don't succeed, failure may be your style.

—*Quentin Crisp*

When people are laughing, they're generally not killing one another.

*—Alan Alda*

Trying to take money out of politics is like trying to take jumping out of basketball.

*—Bill Bradley*

Force and mind are opposites; morality ends where a gun begins.

*—Ayn Rand*

Age is a matter of feeling, not years.

*—Washington Irving*

Don't take on a new personality; it doesn't work.

—*Richard M. Nixon*

The enemy is anybody who's going to get you killed, no matter what side he's on.

—*Joseph Heller*

I think governments are the cancer of civilization.

—*Chuck D.*

We have all known the long loneliness, and we have found the answer is community.

—*Dorothy Day*

Each of us needs something—food, liquor, pot, whatever—
to survive. Dracula needs blood.

—*Frank Langella on his Broadway
and movie role in* Dracula

America wasn't founded so that we could all be better. America was
founded so we could all be anything we damned well pleased.

—*P. J. O'Rourke*

I haven't had sex in eight months. To be honest, I now prefer to
go bowling.

—*Lil' Kim*

A journey is like marriage. The certain way to be wrong is to think you control it.

—*John Steinbeck*

What I wanted to do was to paint sunlight on the side of a house.

—*Edward Hopper*

The worst part of having success is to try and find someone who is happy for you.

—*Bette Midler*

Some of us are becoming the men we wanted to marry.

—*Gloria Steinem*

Bad news isn't wine. It doesn't improve with age.

—*Colin Powell*

There is no female Mozart because there is no female Jack the Ripper.

—*Camille Paglia*

Change your thoughts and you change your world.

—*Norman Vincent Peale*

I belong to an unholy disorder. We call ourselves "Our Lady of Perpetual Astonishment."

—*Kurt Vonnegut*

Happiness is hard to recall. It's just a glow.

—*Frank McCourt*

I am sickened by all religions. Religon has divided people.

—*Howard Stern*

I am at two with nature.

—*Woody Allen*

There is the beauty of light and air, the great scale of the Hudson, majestic in their degree, even at a distance, and announcing still nobler things.

—*Henry James*

I appear to be walking down the street with you, but I'm actually walking in the New York of my mind.

—*David Duchovny*

Gray hair is God's graffiti.

—*Bill Cosby*

I'm spending about $600 a week talking to my analyst. I guess that is the price of success.

—*Robert DeNiro*

If my film makes one more person miserable, I'll feel I've done
my job.

*—Woody Allen*

Freud's stupid. I didn't like Jung or Adler either. I go along with
Samuel Goldwyn: he said anybody who has to see a psychiatrist
ought to have his head examined.

*—Mickey Spillane*

Vote early and vote often.

*—Al Capone*

If you're playing a poker game and you look around the table and you can't tell who the sucker is, it's you.

*—Paul Newman*

I began, in my manner, to make a religion of my neighborhood.

*—Nora Ephron on New Yorkers' obsession with the neighborhoods they live in*

It is no treat being in bed with me.

*—Howard Stern*

When I go I'll take New Year's Eve with me.

*—Guy Lombardo*

Stand up, tall masts of Manhattan! Stand up, beautiful hills of Brooklyn.

*—Walt Whitman*

New York's terrible when somebody laughs on the street very late at night. . . . It makes you feel so lonesome and depressed.

*—Holden Caulfield in J. D. Salinger's*
The Catcher in the Rye

Everything is clearer when you are in love.
                                        —*John Lennon*

〜

They're not looking to meet Mr. Big. They're looking to become Mr. Big.
                        —*Candace Bushnell on women in*
                          *New York circa 2006*

〜

Nail polish . . .
                        —*Jennifer "J. Lo" Lopez when asked*
                          *what she got on her SATs*

〜

Dream as if you'll live forever, live as if you'll die today.

—*James Dean*

The city is thronged with strangers, and everything wears an aspect of intense life.

—*Edgar Allen Poe*

I'm in a war, a cultural war.

—*Howard Stern*

I'm far from being god, but I work goddamn hard.

—*Jay Z*

He was a happy-go-lucky youngster, actually. He studied animals, was often in the zoo, and as we know he was picked up in the Bronx Zoo while playing hooky from school, and I consider that normal also—playing hooky from school. Many boys do this.
    —*Marguerite Oswald on her son Lee Harvey Oswald who lived at 825 East 179th Street in the Bronx in 1953*

Hello from the gutters of NYC, which is filled with dog manure, vomit, stale wine, urine, and blood.
    —*David "Son of Sam" Berkowitz*

. . . If I know fifteen billionaires, I know thirteen unhappy people.
    —*Russell Simmons*

My new motto is: When you're through changing, you're through.

—*Martha Stewart*

If anyone ever said I was not a New Yorker it would break my heart.

—*Diahann Carroll*

Money was never a big motivator for me, except as a way to keep score. The real excitement is playing the game.

—*Donald Trump*

There's so much absurdity. Poverty is so absurd.

—*Frank McCourt*

To be an actor you have to be a child.

—*Paul Newman*

A hot dog at the ballpark is better than a steak at the Ritz.

—*Humphrey Bogart*

As usual there is a great woman behind every idiot.

—*John Lennon*

My regret in life is that I am not someone else.

—*Woody Allen*

Die in nature's time. Yield to nature.

—*Don DeLillo*

Just once before I die I want to climb up on a tenement sky
then scatter my ashes there on the Lower East Side.

—*Miguel Piñero*

I would be free to move back to New York City—which was not just
the Big Apple but Cheese Central.

—*Nora Ephron*

It's okay to be crazy, but don't be insane.

—*Sean "P. Diddy" Combs*

People stay married because they want to, not because the doors
are locked.

—*Paul Newman*

When you leave New York, you are astonished at how clean the rest
of the world is. Clean is not enough.

—*Fran Lebowitz*

There's no such thing as good money or bad money, there's
just money.

—*Charles "Lucky" Luciano*

We'll turn Manhattan into an isle of joy.

*—Lorenz Hart*

There are two things I hear—and am aware that I live in the neighborhood of—the roar of the sea and the hum of the city.
*—Henry David Thoreau while living on Staten Island in 1843*

I could serve coffee using my rear as a ledge.

*—Jennifer Lopez*

I tend to place my wife under a pedestal.

*—Woody Allen*

This city sounds like jazz.

*—Shakira*

I didn't claw my way out of the 'hood just 'cause it was something
to do. I know I got a purpose.

*—Curtis "50 Cent" Jackson*

. . . the City of New York with the sky pouring its light onto the
rivers looked like a vision of enlightenment.

*—John Cheever*

In New York freedom looks like too many choices.

*—Bono*

New York is where the future comes to audition.

—*Mayor Ed Koch*

Young singers ask me, "Do I have to live in New York?" I say,
"You can live wherever you want—as long as people think you live
in New York."

—*Benita Valente*

Out of the tenements Cold as stone,
Dark figures start for work,
I watch them sadly shuffle on,
'Tis dawn, dawn in New York.

—*Claude McKay*

Here's to New York City: the biggest small town in the world.
                    —*John Mellencamp at a concert in Madison Square Garden
                            as he introduced his song "Small Town"*

～

There's no radio station in New York City where you can hear
Sinatra sing, "New York, New York."

                                            —*Hugh Panelo*

# VIII

# THE
# OUTER
# BOROUGHS

I like to think of all the city microcosms so nicely synchronized though unaware of one another . . .

—*A. J. Liebling*

. . . proximity makes elusiveness harder to justify. I am of that small group of brownstone Brooklyn seventies kids.

—*Amy Sohn*

. . . comparing the Brooklyn that I know with Manhattan is like comparing a comfortable and complacent duenna to her more brilliant and neurotic sister.

—*Carson McCullers*

. . . the Wild Things are—lumpish creatures who roll their eyes and gnash their teeth, and were based on Maurice Sendak's own relatives in Brooklyn.

—*Cynthia Zahn*

Alan Harding opened a restaurant on Smith St. called Patois, and the honkeys came out to play.

—*Amy Sohn*

Bed-Stuy is the kind of neighborhood where the only people with money are drug dealers, people who hit the daily number; and people who got hit by cars, sued, and got paid.

—*Chris Rock*

Brooklyn Heights: the dusk of Gods.

—*James Agee*

But ultimately a Brooklyn girl is a homegirl. She knows everyone on the block.

—*Rosie Perez*

Dreaming my way back to Brooklyn . . . is a necessary part of loving it for me—continuing also to love it from afar.

—*Jonathan Lethem*

Eppolito had a handy tag for the kinds of people who weren't
making Brooklyn any safer . . . "three P's—perps, pussies, and pencil
pushing prigs."

*—Ben McGrath*

I hereby prophesy that in 1900 A.D., Brooklyn will be the city and
New York will be the suburb.

*—George Templeton Strong*

I think when people turned on the television, when we marched
in Howard Beach and Bensonhurst, and saw people holding water-
melons and calling people niggers—they never imagined that could
happen in Brooklyn.

*—Al Sharpton*

If even half of the healers were for real, the air over Brooklyn would have been crackling with the concentration of psychic energy.

—*Lara Vapnyar*

In Brooklyn everyone was funny.

—*Jackie Gleason*

More people enter Red Hook than leave it, and those who are not loquacious are the likeliest to leave.

—*H. P. Lovecraft*

Now a chasm as wide as the human condition allows has opened up on Fourth Avenue in Sunset Park . . .

—*Dan Barry*

~

Ocean Parkway is one of Brooklyn's boulevards of happy dreams, gorgeous testimony to the possibility of livable cities.

—*Thomas Oliphant*

~

Robert Moses hated Coney Island. He wanted to wipe out the private amusement area. He tried to get the Cyclone torn down . . . I fought him all the way because I felt Coney Island had a place in New York.

—*Murray Handwerker*

~

Serene was a word you could put to Brooklyn, New York, especially in the summer of 1912. Somber, as a word, was better.

—*Betty Smith*

The famous chip on the shoulder remains an essential part of Brooklyn's character.

—*Thomas Oliphant*

The nighttime air at Coney Island smells like corn dogs and fried clams and a little bit like garbage. It's a good smell once you get used to it, and a good place. There are lights and activity and you never know who's going to walk past. For an old man who's kind of curious, but also kind of not interested in talking to anyone, it's perfect.

—*Neal Pollack*

The stoops of my father's Brooklyn childhood capture my imagination more than the modern skyscrapers of midtown. Our twenty-first-century culture is shoddy and graceless.

—*David Leibowitz*

There are a lot of places to hide in Brooklyn . . . and a lot of people to hide among.

—*Brian Berger*

What's unsettling is to put Manhattan at your back and face the borough. Up from the canyon floor, out of the deep well of streets, gazing out into the Brooklyn Beyond.

—*Jonathan Lethem*

He'd get lost if he tried to find his way back to New York from her neighborhood. Brooklyn was tricky that way. You had to live there in order to find your way about.

*—Betty Smith*

I am a patriot—of the 14th Ward in Brooklyn, where I was raised. The rest of the United States doesn't exist for me, except as idea, or history, or literature.

*—Henry Miller*

In Red Hook, Brooklyn policeman despair of order or reform, and seek rather to erect barriers protecting the outside world from the contagion.

*—H. P. Lovecraft*

Manhattan makes it and Brooklyn takes it.

—*Brooklyn thug motto*

Map or no map, yuh ain't gonna get to know Brooklyn wit no map.

—*Thomas Wolfe*

If you're a young man in East New York,
here's a simple fact of life:
If they don't shoot you with a gun,
they'll cut you with a knife.

—*Cornelius Eady*

The skyscrapers of the city were a collection of hard-ons zeroing in on Brooklyn.

—*Joe Flaherty*

The true aristocrats of Brooklyn are those who sacrifice all for others.

—*Michael Daly*

You don't like my Brooklyn attitude? Stop talking to me.

—*T-shirt on a woman on Greenpoint Avenue, Brooklyn*

God's mercy on the Wild Ginger Man!
> —*Bronx native, J. P. Donleavy, who moved to Ireland
> to write* The Ginger Man, *which spawned
> quite a few Irish pubs in NYC*

I was haunted always by my other life—my drab room in the Bronx,
my square foot of subway . . .
> —*F. Scott Fitzgerald*

I'm a muggy fly-filled day inside a Bronx courtyard and reeking of
diapers, mice filled glue traps . . .
> —*Gil Fagiani*

There it is, ladies and gentlemen, the Bronx is burning!
        —*Howard Cosell during a TV World Series
        broadcast at Yankee Stadium in October 1977*

⌢

When people think of black history in New York City, they think of Harlem or Bed-Stuy, but there was a whole culture of strivers in the South Bronx.
                                    —*Professor Mark Naison*

⌢

"Have you met this wonderful creature yet? She's from the Bronx— the South Bronx. Amazing! Is anybody still living there?"
"No, nobody important . . . just people."
                                    —*Migdalia Cruz*

⌢

. . . it was Pelham Bay that set me shouting, "There's a park for you!"
The entire city could go there, hold a cyclopean picnic, and have
plenty of room to turn around in.

—*James Huneker*

I've got a few dreamers here who are motivated to get out of the
Bronx, but for most of them, English is a second language, and a very
foreign one at that.

—*Linda Fairstein*

The Bronx is more than the sum total of its tragedies.

—*Professor Mark Naison*

The Bronx? No Thonx!

—*Ogden Nash*

There were many bad neighborhoods in New York, but the South
Bronx was a byword for 'slum'. There was no renaissance in its past,
like Harlem, nor signs of gentrification or renewal . . .

—*Edward Conlon*

Wasn't any one of us going to get out? The Bronx—where people
talk with such intriguing accents.

—*Migdalia Cruz*

Whatever our differences, we agreed that the Cross-Bronx Expressway, a deep, eternally sluggish river of brake lights and diesel exhaust coursing through a waste of twisted rebar and abandoned scrap, is as gruesome a stretch of highway as exists in these parts.

—*Nick Paumgarten*

Not much interest is paid to where the poor folks go. In New York it's often the borough of Queens, where so far in the city's history has remained resolutely unhip and uncolonized.

—*John Strausbaugh*

Whatever else you say about John Gotti, he kept the neighborhood up.

—*Maria Rescigna*

[As a Latino family] . . . we upgraded to a poor all-Irish neighborhood in Sunnyside, Queens, where we were like pioneers. Manifest
Destiny in reverse.

*—John Leguizamo*

. . . the present day Ellis Island—Jackson Heights, Queens. Our
tenement building was like a modern Tower of Babel.

*—John Leguizamo*

After twenty-five years of living in Queens as geographic
undesirables, we know that "Let's get together soon," really means,
"Let's get together soon—in Manhattan."

*—Barbara Williams Cosentino*

All the way through the Queens-Midtown Tunnel, I wept for the city
I'd missed.

—*Rene Steinke*

Edward Villella . . . danced with the New York City ballet in the
sixties and seventies . . . arguably the first home-grown male star
of American classical dance . . . he looked like a local product. He
was a street kid from Queens—tough, virile, and cocky.

—*Joan Acocella*

I'm Corona under the shadows of Shea Stadium, where brown men
became famous and moved to Long Island.

—*Bushra Rehman*

I'm Corona, home of all those old time World's Fair relics in Flushing Meadows. . . . Some ancient tribe of white people lived here long ago. I'm the Stonehenge . . . made from time when New York City . . . was imagining the world's future.

—*Bushra Rehman*

In Astoria you've got families of immigrants, proud people, hard-working people. Manhattan kids are straight out of a music video.

—*L. B. Deyo*

Osama bin Laden can kiss my royal Irish ass. . . . And I live in Rockaway, bitch.

—*Mike Moran, FDNY*

People born in Queens, raised to say each morning they get on the
subway and go to "the city," have a resentment of Manhattan, of the
swiftness of its life and the success of the people who live there.

—*Jimmy Breslin*

The city seen from the Queensboro Bridge is always the city seen
for the first time, in its first wild promise of all the mystery and the
beauty in the world.

—*F. Scott Fitzgerald*

Tourism in Queens is a road less traveled . . . nobody knows
about Queens.

—*Terri Osborne*

You know what they call sushi out in the Rockaways? Bait.

*—John Daly*

By far the least populated and most remote borough of New York City, Staten Island is often the object of ridicule by outsiders. It can be enigmatic, easy to overlook and forgotten.

*—Steve Maluk*

Staten Island had always been the most isolated, the most ignored of New York's five boroughs; it was separated from Manhattan by five miles of water and a half hour's ride on the ferry.

*—Gay Talese*

Staten Island is the Australia of New York City.

—*Dave Hollander*

Nothing has ever been successful in Staten Island in its entire history. The only thing that might save this island is a lot of new people.

—*Robert Regan*

Rafik Abboud's little acre and a half is not quite the end of the earth, not quite the end of Staten Island. But it's close.

—*Andy Newman*

The Staten Island Ferry, the world's greatest bargain when it was a nickel—today it's free—carries over 18 million passengers a year.

—*Steve Maluk*

The Hamptons? You're still not caught up in that, are you? Darling . . . the Hamptons are over.

—*Candace Bushnell*

# IX

# WHAT IS NEW YORK?

My favorite city in the world is New York. Sure it's dirty—but like a beautiful lady smoking a cigar.

—*Joan Rivers*

The city is mutable, so constantly changing that it's almost impossible to get a fix on it. . . . Simply put, New York never gets boring. Anything can happen here.

—*Cheryl Farr Leas*

New York is the most fatally fascinating thing in America. She sits like a Great Witch at the gate of the country.

—*James Weldon Johnson*

No other American city is so intensely American as New York.
—*Anthony Trollope*

Hell's a mild climate. This is Hell's Kitchen, no less.
—*An unnamed police officer in 1880s New York*

New York is Baghdad on the subway.
—*O. Henry*

I miss the animal buoyancy of New York, the animal vitality. I did not mind that it had no meaning and no depth.
—*Anais Nin*

In New York, their eyes pop as they spell out Apocalypse.
*—John Dos Passos*


Broadway. . . . Nowhere else do the Lord and the Devil work so nearly side by side.
*—Jack Lait and Lee Mortimer*


. . . New York University started using my name in ads for the school and I said in an interview, "That's odd, cause they didn't like my film and they didn't give me a degree. And then they send me a degree. And with a degree and $1.50 you can buy a cup of coffee in New York."
*—Jim Jarmusch*

Far below and around the city lay like a ragged purple dream . . .

—*O.Henry*

It was a cruel city, but it was a lively one, a savage city, yet it
had such tenderness; a bitter, harsh and violent catacomb of
stone and steel . . . roaring, fighting a constant ceaseless warfare
of men and machinery . . .

—*Thomas Wolfe*

At its best New York was a city of accidental epiphanies.

—*Pat Conroy*

New York has always been going to hell but somehow it never gets there.

—*Robert Persig*

In New York, boy, money really talks—I'm not kidding.

—*J. D. Salinger*

New York had all the iridescence of the beginning of the world.

—*F. Scott Fitzgerald*

New York, thy name is paranoia.

—*Stephen King*

City of glorious days,
Of hope, and labour and mirth,
With room and to spare on thy splendid bays
For the ships of all the earth.

—*Richard Watson Gilder*

New York makes one think of the collapse of civilization, about
Sodom and Gomorrah, the end of the world. The end wouldn't
come as a surprise here. Many people already bank on it.

—*Saul Bellow*

The present in New York is so powerful that the past is lost.
                    —*John Jay Chapman*, 1898

It is a miracle that New York works at all. The whole thing
is implausible.
                              —*E. B. White*

It's true that what you find in New York is something other than
America. Only small towns and small countries are self-satisfied;
a real capital goes beyond its borders.
                         —*Simone de Beauvoir*

New York was an inexhaustible space, a labyrinth of endless steps, and no matter how far he walked, no matter how well he came to know its neighborhoods and streets, it always left him with the feeling of being lost.

*—Paul Aster*

Then there came a time . . . when you could not find sin in Times Square, save for the mortal sin of mediocrity; a time when you could not find an ashtray in a bar; a time when real life and real freedom, replaced by lip service to them, became the vice that New York, like the vast dying nothingness of America itself, was ashamed to mention.

*—Nick Tosches*

What is barely hinted at in other American cities is condensed and enlarged in New York.

*—Saul Bellow*

New York is the focus, the point where American and European interests converge.

*—Margaret Fuller*

Of cities I know, New York wins the paranoia award.

*—David Lehman*

The City. See, that's what we call it. The rest of the world calls it the Apple. . . . We call it the City and let it go at that.

—*Lawrence Block*

New York is a city where children of all colors can dance.

—*G. N. Miller*

Living in New York City is all about insulating yourself from the outside world.

—*Bruce Hinton*

New York, the nation's thyroid gland.

—*Christopher Morley*

The only people who can afford to live in New York are the rich and the poor.

—*David McGlynn*

One of the special characteristics of New York is that it is different from a London or a Paris because it's the financial capital, and the cultural capital, but not the political capital.

—*Ron Chernow*

Los Angeles is just New York lying down.

*—Quentin Crisp*

When it's three o' clock in New York, it's still 1938 in London.

*—Bette Midler*

During many a single week . . . more money is spent in New York upon useless and evil things that would suffice to run Denmark for a year.

*—H. L. Mencken*

I think that New York is not the cultural centre of America, but the business and administrative centre of American culture.

—*Saul Bellow*

It is ridiculous to set a detective story in New York City. New York City is itself a detective story.

—*Agatha Christie*

There is more sophistication and less sense in New York than anywhere else on the globe.

—*Don Herold*

Not only is New York City the nation's melting pot, it is also the casserole, the chafing dish, and the charcoal pit.

—*Mayor John V. Lindsay*

If London is a watercolor, New York is an oil painting.

—*Peter Shaffer*

Living as you do in New York, the navel of the universe, it is easy to confuse the Midwest and the South.

—*John Fleischman*

New York is a sucked orange.

—*Ralph Waldo Emerson*

New York is not Mecca. It just smells like it.

—*Neil Simon*

Hemingway described literary New York as a battlefield of tapeworms trying to feed on each other.

—*John Updike*

The fact that New York continues in the face of the chaos, of the crime, of the madness, you just think that it would just pop and vanish, just explode.

—*Spalding Gray*

In New York you can have anything you want, and even in the old days you could, too, so that hasn't changed.

—*Brooke Astor*

Although New York was the best target because it represents to bin Laden all the things that are wrong with the West, it is also better equipped to handle something like that.

—*Charles Stone*

The city makes you want more. I travel the world, but find my real inspiration comes from New York.

*—James Kieran Pine*

New York, that concert of the expensively provisional.

*—Henry James*

New York glorified in the self-given title of "Metropolis," Greek for "Mother City."

*—John Mulligan*

With the New York media, it's either going to be good or bad and nothing in between.

—*Mike Heimerdinger*

For a while, almost five years ago, Manhattan was, in fact, an isle of the dead.

—*Peter Schjeldahl on the aftermath of 9/11 on New York City*

MAMMON, n. The God of the world's leading religion. The chief temple is in the holy city of New York.

—*Ambrose Bierce*

In its tough, often remorseless way, New York is a crucible for every manner of talent.

—*Pete Hamill*

The solution to world hunger lies on the streets of New York.

—*Adam Weissman*

In New York, we are so frequently within earshot of strangers. We constantly find ourselves smack in someone else's drama.

—*William Meyers*

Manhattan has nonchalance about the world and itself known nowhere else.

*—Jack Lait and Lee Mortimer*


Nobody ever accuses New York of approximating serenity.

*—Bob Brody*


New York is the dream world, the center of jazz and rock.

*—Gyorgy Ligeti*

Hustling didn't seem like one of the options; it seemed like the only option.

—*Curtis "50 Cent" Jackson*

Hip-hop was not created based on hatred. It was created at giant block parties in the Bronx and Harlem, based on a very innocent notion of urban creative expression.

—*Kabir Sen*

. . . in some respects New York is more set in its provincialism than any hick town in America.

—*Josephus Dasels*

New York is cocaine, opium, hashish.

—*Ambrose Bierce*

I still haven't figured out how New York works. . . . But it does work, when logically a city of 8.2 million people from everywhere should be dysfunctional.

—*Joyce Purnick*

New York is a city of daily irritation, occasional horrors, hourly tests of will and even courage, and huge dollops of pure beauty.

—*Pete Hamill*

When I was growing up New York was safe, everything was either cheap or free, and, in midtown, no gays, no blacks, no women. Now the city is violent, everything costs the earth, and we are all visible.

—*Vivian Gornick*

Harlem, I came to feel, was the shining transcendence of a national negative.

—*Ralph Ellison*

It seems the oldest city in the world. Tho they are new in it.

—*George Oppen*

New York thrives on imagination and reinvention. Ever-changing, it is more idea than place.

—*Joyce Purnick*

It showed me the poetry that was inherent in the chaff of the street. . . . There was something quite elevated in the way people spoke.

—*Clifford Odet*

It is here in the dirt and the smells and the heat that New York must struggle to keep a critical part of its city from falling apart.

—*Jimmy Breslin*

New York has a life of its own, its own pulse, which beats just a bit faster than that of its inhabitants.

—*Uri Savir*

If it's more than a New York minute, it's too long.

—*Sigrid Nunez*

The great days in New York were just before you got there.

—*Lewis Gannett*

New York has a trip-hammer vitality which drives you insane with
restlessness, if you have no inner stabilizer.

—*Henry Miller*

Broadway has become "a staggering machine of desire"
unequaled everywhere.

—*Jerome Charyn*

This is a city of smokers. This is a city of cell phones.

—*David Crowe*

If a single Catholic church is burned in New York, the city will become a second Moscow.

—*Archbishop John "Dagger" Hughes*

Whatever the urge, there is a place New Yorkers can go to satisfy it —a series of vices are hidden in plain sight.

—*Clemente Lisi*

New York is the place where all the aspirations of the Western World meet to form one vast master aspiration as powerful as the suction of a steam dredge.

—*H. L. Mencken*

New York, the capsized city, half-capsized, anyway, with the inhabitants hanging on, most of them still able to laugh as they cling to their island that is their life's predicament.

—*Maeve Brennan*

A map of the city, colored to designate nationalities, would show more stripes than on a zebra, and more colors than a rainbow.

—*Jacob Riis*

Here in New York it's always feast or famine.

—*Larry Silverstein*

New York: the empress queen of this vast continent.

*—Alan Melville*

New York was the best place to feel the power of the young nation coiled for release.

*—Andrew Delbanco*

New York has always been the face the country showed the world.

*—L. B. Deyo*

While other places tend to get stuck, New York continues to evolve.

*—Karl Lagerfeld*

The great advantage to New York is. . . . It's inspirational as an artist—and you don't even necessarily need to do anything but just be here. It keeps you interested.

*—Matt Dillon*

There are 25,000 opium smokers in the city of New York alone. At one time there were two great colonies, one in the Tenderloin, one of course in Chinatown.

*—Stephen Crane, 1896*

This town seems to me to have other alleged metropolises skinned to flag stations.

—*O. Henry*

The city would not give and stood defiant.

—*Paul Rosenfeld*

New York is a setting for a drama that is being played, a spectacle which is being rehearsed.

—*Stephen Graham*

. . . the inner tragedies, no matter how intense, are viewed through the tawdry lace of New York.

—*Dawn Powell*

New York, of course, just isn't America.

—*A. J. Liebling*

As soon as you feel you understand New York, an unpalatable fact becomes apparent: your understanding is obsolete.

—*John Gattuso*

In the shadows of the city waits an invisible frontier—a wilderness, thriving in the deep places, woven through dead storm drains and live subway tunnels, coursing over third rails.

—*L.B. Deyo*

# COMING
*TO*
# NEW YORK

The people they met in Manhattan seemed to have no past. . . . It was as though their parents were imposters, primitive custodians who had kidnapped these princes and princesses of the shimmering night from their rightful realm.

*—Joe Flaherty*

Seeing with my innocent road-eyes the absolute madness and fantastic hooair of New York with its millions and millions hustling forever for a buck among themselves.

*—Jack Kerouac*

A city like this one makes me dream tall and feel in on things.

*—Toni Morrison*

The city always stimulated some long dormant gland of self improvement when I crossed her rivers.

—*Pat Conroy*

What am I always listening for in Harlem? A voice that says, "This is your place, too" . . . the accents are unfamiliar; all my New York kin are dead.

—*Elizabeth Alexander*

The original poor of the Lower East Side had scuffled without hope, of course, selling their labor for low wages. Their children fled to Queens or Jersey, leaving room in the tenements for middle-class children loosely defined as "artists."

—*Joyce Johnson*

Curb Your God.

—*T-shirt slogan seen on a New York street in 2006*

Sometimes I get bored riding down the beautiful streets of L.A. I know it sounds crazy, but I just want to go to New York and see people suffer.

—*Donna Summer*

I would never feel good enough for New York, but I would always feel better if I was at least taking steps to measure up to her eminent standards.

—*Pat Conroy*

New York, like family, will always take you back.

—*Cynthia Ceilan*

I've always felt an ineluctable guilt when I was just taking it easy in New York.

—*Pat Conroy*

Talent tends to cluster.

—*William Goldman*

You see I was in a curious position in New York: it never occurred to me that I was living a real life there. In my imagination I was always there for just another few months. . . . For that reason I was most comfortable in the company of Southerners. They seemed to be in New York as I was, on some indefinitely extended leave from wherever they belonged . . . temporary exiles.

—*Joan Didion*

If you're not in New York, you're camping out.

*—Thomas E. Dewey*

I sit in one of the dives on Fifty Second Street uncertain and afraid. . . . As the clever hopes expire of a low and dishonest decade.

*—W. H. Auden*

One belongs to New York instantly, one belongs to it as much in five minutes as in five years.

*—Thomas Wolfe*

Once you have lived in New York and it has become your home, no place else is good enough.

*—John Steinbeck*

I am a flygirl with a new haircut in New York City in a mural that is dying everyday.

—*Elizabeth Alexander*

For where does one run to when he's already in the Promised Land?

—*Claude Brown*

For was not his very plunging into the polyglot abyss of New York's underworld a freak beyond sensible explanation?

—*H. P. Lovecraft*

New York, this city of ambition, is brutal, unrelenting, neurotic. If you're willing to take a chance and pay the price, you can get what you want here.

—*Ed Hayes*

You should heed my advice on surviving in New York. It's simple. Always walk in the middle of the street. That way you can see where it is going to come from.

—*Noel Edwards*

New York is the portal of the American Dream. People come here to start their lives. But if you go and the portal is closed . . . you fall much further down.

—*Jack Matthews*

New York is the place you come to when you don't belong anywhere else.

—*Cynthia Ceilan*

New Yorkers panic if anything about the Midwest comes into conversation, because one, they don't know anything about it and, two, they're not absolutely sure where it is.

—*Garrison Keillor*

New York is still a white man's city. The Chinese and Latinos that come here, even they want to be white. A lot of black folks just live here. That don't make it theirs.

—*John Jeffery*

A car is useless in New York, essential everywhere else. The same with good manners.

—*Mignon McLaughlin*

Living in New York absolutely never requires a writer to live outside his language. On the contrary: the mother tongue is enriched with all the variants that the enormous Spanish-speaking community of this city have contributed to the language.

*—Dionisio Canas*

. . . those that live in New York find it absurd that there should be any debate regarding English as the official language of the U.S. Most people view it perfectly natural that, in Manhattan, one is surrounded by the sounds of hundreds of different languages.

*—Dionisio Canas*

In the dark all men were the same color. In the dark our fellow man was seen more clearly than in the normal light of a New York night.

*—Stephen Kennedy*

The mania started with insomnia and not eating and being driven,
driven to find an apartment, driven to see everybody, driven to do
New York, driven to never shut up.

— *Patty Duke*

We're a thoughtful people. We are not New Yorkers.

— *Garrison Keillor*

When I came to New York in 1980, the sense of danger was
externalized. It was on the streets. Everyone I know except me
was mugged on a regular basis. . . . I feel like we lost something
when this city became so safe: You couldn't locate the edge.

— *Jay McInerny*

When I came to New York it was like a whole new world was opened—I felt like everything going on in New York had been kept secret from me.

—*Laurie Simmons*

When I came to New York people immediately accepted me in the sense that I was anonymous. And I liked that.

—*Patti Smith*

I think of the sights and sounds and mad rushes of fear sensation that come over you all at once when you are in New York.

—*John Pickett*

If we took all of our coming to New York stories and placed them
on a grid, I suspect we would find that we are all located somewhere
between home and exile.

—*Karen H. Senecal*

New York is my Lourdes, where I go for spiritual refreshment . . .
a place where you're least likely to be bitten by a wild goat.

—*Brendan Behan*

I knew I couldn't live in America and I wasn't ready to move
to Europe, so I moved to an island off the coast of America—
New York City.

—*Spalding Gray*

I moved to New York City for my health. I'm paranoid and it was the only place where my fears were justified.

—*Anita Weiss*

I love short trips to New York, to me it is the finest three-day town on earth.

—*James Cameron*

I do believe that those of us who live in New York have a profound understanding of the fragility of life itself. The biggest part of preparing to live in New York is . . . to live in a very concrete way . . . that everything . . . is temporary.

—*Karen H. Senecal*

When I was in the service I got tired of defending New York. I would tell them if you don't like it don't come. Who wants to see Picasso? Who wants good Chinese food at 3 a.m.? Stay in Indiana if you like it so much.

*—Edward Volpe*

New York is spontaneous. New York is out of control. Still, we come on rafts, life boats, schooners, surfboards and water skis because we desire to live beyond our sensible selves.

*—Karen H. Senecal*

Never let the poor and destitute emigrant stop at New York—it will be his ruin.

*—Calvin Coltin*

Though one can dine in New York, one could not dwell.

—*Oscar Wilde*

I think of New York as puree and the rest of the United States as vegetable soup.

—*Spalding Gray*

New York was a relief—not all hierarchical and rule bound [like Japan].

—*Ayumi Hamasaki*

You can never get lost in New York, as long as you keep moving, but you can get stuck sometimes. It depends on your stamina more than your sense of direction.

*—Edward Conlon*

The horror and the heat a New York City firefighter faces throughout his career is a filmmaker's dream.

*—Russell Feliciano*

I'm on deck the dawn we sail into New York. I'm sure I'm in a film that will end and the lights will come up in the Lyric Cinema.

*—Frank McCourt*

Puerto Ricans . . . they hit New York in the 1940s, the wrong time. But like when is it right, when your face don't help, your accent ain't French, and your clothes don't fit?

—*Edwin Torres*

You can have a great life in New York as long as you don't weaken.

—*Dr. Edward Malloy*

New York lets you be yourself, and that is why I stayed.

—*Gavin Schmidt*

New York is like a carnival on Devil's Island. At some point, everyone who lives here says, ' I'm gonna escape. . . . But first I'm gonna take one more spin on the Tilt-O-Whirl . . .' In the end, no one ever gets away.

—*Jim Knipfel*

More than elsewhere, everybody here wants to be somebody.

—*Sydney J. Harris*

They sat behind sewing machines and stood behind steam tables. In other words they busted their asses, they went for the dream.

—*Edwin Torres on the experiences Puerto-Ricans faced when coming to New York after World War II*

In New York my dreams came true and with that all my nightmares also.

—*Laura Benson*

It is easy to hide in New York City. Sometimes it is even easy to get trapped. Ask the cats.

—*Manny Fernandez*

New York is also, at least for those of us who came there from somewhere else, a city for only the very young.

—*Joan Didion*

She was nurse; she was asylum; she was the city itself, with its force and possessiveness. She could be counted on to succor the weak, as she could be counted on to destroy the strong.

*—Louis Auchincloss*

We were happy to be in a city the beauty of which was unknown, uncozy, and not small scale.

*—Edwin Denby*

Down through the years people have been attracted to and repelled by New York. Too huge and powerful to be ignored, the city stirs extreme emotion.

*—Edward Robb Ellis*

There, gaping before us, were the jaws of the iron dragon: the immense New York metropolis.

*—Bernardo Vega*

There are no fountains of eternal youth. Not in New York, anyway. And if there were, somebody'd tear them down.

*—Louis Auchincloss*

. . . I sensed for the first time that people in New York could not possibly be as happy as we used to think they were . . .

*—Bernardo Vega*

. . . heroin had become my sole occupation as well as my one solace in the non-stop clang of a city that clearly had no use for me.

—*Paul Kopasz*

$\backsim$

. . . the awful realization that New York was a city after all and not a universe.

—*F. Scott Fitzgerald*

$\backsim$

In this city, things are not the way they are out there in what is known as the United States.

—*Alan Feuer*

$\backsim$

And so I arrived in New York, without a watch.

—*Bernardo Vega*

Here I was in New York, city of prose and fantasy, of capitalist automation, its streets a triumph of cubism, its moral philosophy that of the dollar . . .

—*Leon Trotsky*

And what is the taste of New York? To much of the world it's cheesecake.

—*Ruth Reichel*

. . . I came to believe the Isle of Manhattan was, in fact, the isle of the City of the Dead.

—*Emily Barton*

Now we understand much more clearly, why people from all over the world want to come to New York and to America. It's called freedom.

—*Rudy Giuliani*

I recently moved to New York to take my dream job. Without the help of my parents I would have never been able to relocate or even consider living here.

—*Anne Walter*

These immigrants came here, I came here, my mother and father came here for a better future.

—*Nick Lombardo*

When New Yorkers said 'train' it meant the subway.

—*Dan Wakefield*

New York was the city of my dreams but now I'm here the dreams are gone and it's not what I expected at all.

—*Frank McCourt*

Instead of a city of silver rivers and golden bridges, America turned out to be Uncle David's flat on Avenue C . . .

—*Kate Simon*

We'd take the Q train into the city and exit at a different stop each time . . . we would experience the city at random, not as tourists but as explorers.

—*Lara Vapnyar*

We're very lucky because New York is a mecca for artists.

—*David Marquis*

Almost all dance companies prosper, when they prosper, by touring. In New York they lose money.

—*Joan Acocella*

I imagined that the city was off limits for me, enclosed by a glass screen; I could admire it, but I couldn't break through.

—*Lara Vapnyar*

What a magnet New York is! Better to be a dishwasher there than a very important person in one's own home town.

—*Langston Hughes*

Send these, the homeless, the tempest-tost to me, I lift my lamp beside the golden door.

—*Emma Lazarus*

Ellis Island represented a traumatic event in the lives of most of the twelve million immigrants who were processed there. It represented a chaotic nightmare.

—*Oscar Israelowitz*

But has it occurred to you that these people are a kind of vampire? See, I think that's why they look so pale and weak. They come to New York and sink their fangs, and they bleed everything white.

—*L. B. Deyo on the trust-fund hipsters who have invaded Manhattan*

And a person who had really been to New York was more wonderful to me than angels.

—*Langston Hughes*

. . . we felt the joy of having "made it," of belonging to this city that we had known only through movies.

—*Lara Vapnyar*

. . . the city is too fluid for prepared itineraries, even if we were diligent enough to make them.

—*L. B. Deyo*

The Statue of Liberty seemed insignificant but the harbour was glorious. There will always be a stinging enchantment for me in this arrival.

—*Noel Coward*

He might as well been in the Gobi Desert, instead of a city of more than eight million far from his homeland. But such is the story of New York City.

—*Rose Kim*

When Ellis Island was operating at full capacity . . . wealthy visitors from Manhattan would come as spectators of the chaotic conditions going on below in the Registry Hall. It was an entertaining spectacle for these rich folks.

—*Oscar Israelowitz*

New York is a very livable city. But when you move away and become a visitor the city seems to turn against you.

—*Nora Ephron*

The thing that interested me then as now about New York . . . was the sharp, and at the same time immense contrast it showed between the dull and the shrewd, the strong and the weak, the rich and the poor, the wise and the ignorant.

*—Theodore Dreiser*

New York is so polygot and international, it becomes easy for the walker-writer to turn a corner and imagine himself in Prague or Montevideo.

*—Phillip Lopate*

We seemed to enter the harbour of New York upon waves of liquid gold . . .

*—Frances Trollope*

New York, indeed, appeared to us, even when we saw it by a soberer light, a lovely and noble city.

*—Frances Trollope*

The Battery on Sunday is the Champ Elysees of foreigners. I heard nothing spoken around me but French and German.

*—Nathaniel Parker Willis*

It was a confusion of tongues, and one wondered where in this cosmopolitan Babel were the authentic Americans.

*—Ernest Duvergier De Hauranne*

I came to New York City and started the *Chinese American*. I
knew nothing of journalism save in a vague way, and went to
work accordingly.

— *Wong Chin Foo*

From the very first moment of arrival at this city of fire, the eye
is blinded.

— *Maxim Gorky*

. . . if you are going to be so weak . . . and let every little thing work
upon you in that way, you'd better not come to New York. You'll see
enough misery here.

— *William Dean Howells*

The Dutch purchased Manhattan . . . from the Indians . . . in 1626 for $24 worth of trinkets. . . . What exactly transpired here? These Indians were not even from Manhattan. They were . . . Carnarsie Indians, from Brooklyn . . . and came upon these . . . settlers who wanted to give them trinkets . . . for land they didn't even own?

—*Oscar Israelowitz*

The city hums with its constant, insatiate, hungry roar.

—*Maxim Gorky*

You can settle yourselves in a hundred different ways in New York; that is one merit of the place.

—*William Dean Howells*

. . . little Ellis Island, the first harbour of refuge and stage of patience for the millions or so of immigrants annually knocking at our official door.

—*Henry James*

. . . this was really my first visit to New York; and as I walked about that evening I began to feel the dread power of the city . . .

—*James Weldon Johnson*

. . . one could not break with New York. If one floated aimlessly about inside its walls, within them one remained.

—*Paul Rosenfeld*

Solitary walking along the empty streets seems to attune the mind
to the city.

*—Stephen Graham*

In a matter of decades, New York has recast itself as a new American
polestar, where crime rates are low, welfare is closely policed and
smoking and honking carry fines.

*—Michael Brick*

I felt that no actuality could live up to my expectations of New
York's splendor.

*—F. Scott Fitzgerald*

New York blends the gift of privacy with the excitement of participation. On any person who desires such queer prizes, New York will bestow the gift of loneliness and the gift of privacy.

—*E. B. White*

There are too many interruptions in Manhattan . . . the whole social and political situation. But one has to find a way to do both, to be private and involved in civil rights.

—*James Baldwin*

# LIBERTY
*AND*
## JUSTICE
*FOR*
## ALL?

I am the Statue of Liberty. . . . I want to mate with the Golden Gate and birth renewed civil liberties so once again America will be land of the brave, home of the free.

*—Tsauraa Litzky*

The City of New York is an enormous citadel, a modern Carcassonne. Walking between the magnificent skyscrapers one feels the presence on the fringe of a howling, raging mob, a mob with empty bellies, a mob unshaven and in rags.

*—Henry Miller*

I've told you how I got rich by honest graft. Now, let me tell you most politicians who are accused of robbin' the city get rich the same way.

*—G. W. Plunkitt*

The courts in New York are like meat grinders of people's souls. No one comes out undamaged.

*—Ernie Koy*

~

This is New York and there's no law against being annoying.

*—William Kuntsler*

~

There are three things a man must do alone: be born, die, and testify.

*—New York City Mayor Jimmy Walker in 1932*

~

New York produced the only serial killer, the Son of Sam, who knew how to use a semicolon in a letter.

*—Jimmy Breslin*

~

It is far preferable to fight them in the streets of Baghdad than in the streets of New York (where the residents would immediately surrender).

*—Ann Coulter on her disdain of liberal New Yorkers*

Well, there are certain sections of New York, Major, that I wouldn't advise you to invade.

*—Humphrey Bogart as Rick in* Casablanca

New York is a mess. The poor are having a harder and harder time. A lot of it stems from drugs—I believe in legalization.

*—William F. Buckley*

In a New York court case you know the verdict was fair when all sides are unhappy with the outcome.

*—Judge Richard A. Goldberg*

My only regret with Timothy McVeigh is he did not go to the New York Times building.

*—Ann Coulter*

The knife of corruption endangered the life of New York City. The scalpel of the laws is making us well again.

*—New York City Mayor Edward I. Koch*

The only thing on the level in the court system in New York is the water in the toilet bowls.

—*Judge Michael Feinberg*

In Hell's Kitchen the living tended to forget about the dead before the bodies were cold.

—*Jeffery Deaver*

You write for the New York press? Then I guess I better watch what I say.

—*President George W. Bush*

Skepticism has been replaced with shrugged shoulders as New Yorkers accept less freedom to preserve the appearance of freedom.
—*Billy Gorta*

If I am a bad Catholic, I shall be punished by Someone I fear far more than the New York Catholic voter.
—*William F. Buckley*

New York is a different country. Maybe it ought to have a separate government. Everybody thinks differently, acts differently.
—*Henry Ford*

Every day in New York City is a more dangerous place to live than the day before.

—*Mayor John V. Lindsay*

They couldn't touch nothing without a warrant. Anyone grew up in Harlem learned that with their mother's milk.

—*S. J. Rozan*

Anyway, New York is to Bush a bit like what Berlin was to Hitler, isn't it? I mean the place where he's least popular.

—*Alan Bennett*

This city was built on loopholes.

—*Justin Scott*

He is under arrest. I am charging him with DWC. You know what DWC means in New York City? Driving While Chinese.

*—An unnamed female NYPD officer*

I am the man who stood alone at Madison Square Garden all by my-self denouncing Louis Farrakhan for calling Judaism a gutter religion.

*—Mayor David Dinkins*

Basically, stealing for all practical purposes might as well be legal in New York.

*—Mike Judge*

Morever, New York, located in the very heart of the Northern States, is the place where the President meets with the most violent opposition.

—*Ernest Duvergier de Hauranne*

But Hillary [Rodham Clinton] had a gigantic problem to overcome: her penchant for secrets and concealment would not sit well with New Yorkers.

—*Edward Klein*

In New York City we need police officers to protect even the dead.

—*William Dean*

It's a time when the entire city of New York comes together, gathers in that huge hole . . . calling off the names of those who died in the infamous attack that changed America . . . changed the world.

—*John Hood on the mourners who gather at Ground Zero*

As a congressman you make peanuts, as a mayor you can become a millionaire.

—*Hugh Addonizio*

[Mayor Bloomberg] shares my conviction for standing up for the most vulnerable, which here in New York means building a city that works for everyone.

—*Fernando Ferrer*

This is the first election in New York City history where the majority is the minority.

—*Hank Sheinkopf on the 2005 mayoral election*

Al Sharpton. . . . He's managed to annoy just about everyone on the New York political scene, while demonstrating an uncanny ability to drag his issues onto the public stage.

—*Dwight Garner*

The city functions on the lubrication of mutual indifference.

—*Carolyn Wheat*

The Giuliani Administration in New York City is like the Alps.
The higher you go the whiter it gets.

*—Reverend Al Sharpton*

Sooner or later, a thug will tale his tale. We all want to go on the
record. So let's hear it for the hoods. The Jews out of Brownsville.
The Blacks on Lenox. The Italians from Mulberry.

*—Edwin Torres*

Wasn't any of that brotherhood jive in them days. Git that Po' Rican!
We was catchin' hell.

*—Edwin Torres*

By September 10, 2001, Rudolph Giuliani seemed to have worn out his welcome as Mayor of New York, but the sorrier aspects of his two terms of office were all but wiped from the collective memory by his aplomb amidst the chaos of 9/11.

*—Richard Brody*

You have to rule by compromise in this city or you will get nothing done.

*—Mayor Robert F. Wagner*

The urban crisis that New York . . . suffered helped discredit liberalism in the eyes of many Americans.

*—Vincent J. Cannato on the*
*New York of the late 1960s*

Sure I can beat him. Who ever heard of a Republican winning in
New York City?

> —*Mayor Robert F. Wagner in 1965 before
> losing to Republican John V. Lindsay*

[It] is considered [in New York City] far less extraordinary that
a criminal should break a law, than that a criminal should be
apprehended for doing so.

> —*William F. Buckley*

I fear that a part of the failure to deal successfully with crime in
New York is a result of the unfortunate breakdown in relationships
between the police and a substantial part of the people of our city.

> —*Mayor John V. Lindsay*

Politics in New York is not for the weak.

—*Luigi Marano*

If you elect a matinee-idol mayor, you're going to get a musical-comedy administration.

—*Robert Moses on Mayor John V. Lindsay*

We are the lucky possessors of a city order that makes it relatively simple to keep the peace because there are plenty of eyes on the street.

—*Jane Jacobs*

The poor do not count in this city. They have no clout.

—*Herman Badillo*

Violence—that's the only thing this city understands.

—*Willie Smith*

You just wanted to stop the riot, so you beat up the looters with ax handles and nightsticks. You beat 'em and left them in the street.

—*Former cop Robert Knightly on the*
*1977 blackout looting riots in Brooklyn*

Welcome to City Hall, or my crib, as I like to call it. Not everybody here understands our language.

—*Mayor Mike Bloomberg*

I'm running for mayor of New York City. I've got to relate to all people.

—*Percy Sutton*

Gracias, New York! . . . Take heart. A new city is rising. Our time is now.

—*Fernando Ferrer*

Only suckers try to double-cross Broadway, and it always ends up in one-way tickets out of town.

—*Colson Whitehead*

For me what has happened politically in New York City, stays in New York City.

—*Kurt Andersen*

It's one of those things in New York, the world's richest city;
hundreds of thousands of its people do not have enough to eat.

—*Albor Ruiz*

I think that New York City lived with a kind of unspoken
compromise from the New Deal until the 1990's that balanced
out many interests.

—*William Bryk*

I will do thirty years before transit workers surrender. Working
people have tried to obey the law, and we have gotten nothing
but insults for it.

—*Roger Toussaint, President, TWU Local 100, the day he
entered jail on a ten-day sentence for the 2005 transit strike*

New York City is its own universe: a cauldron of competing politicians and interest groups.

—*Hillary Rodham Clinton*

The problem in New York is too much crime, not too much police brutality.

—*William F. Buckley*

People say, "Oh, wow, in Thailand people buy and sell children." I can show you four places in Brooklyn where people buy children.

—*Kate Mullen, legal aid lawyer*

The more time you spend in the courthouse, the smaller New York's underworld came to seem.

*—Ben McGrath on the 2006 Mafia cops trial*

There's a place for gambling. There's a place for neighborhood.

*—Lawyer Bruce Cutler*

When it gets mad, the upper Upper West Side springs fiercely into combat—most of the time, that is.

*—Joseph Berger*

The beatings will continue without the proof of innocence.

*—Seen on an NYPD officer's duty bag*

As someone once told me, New York would be a great city if they ever completed it.

—*Mayor David Dinkins*

Sell, buy, or use fireworks—we cannot replace your eyes, your hands, or your life. We can arrest you. We can confiscate your car or close your business.

—*NYPD flyer handed out around July 4th*

I had a prisoner in Brooklyn Supreme Court who was fighting with the other officers. I asked him why he was so angry. He said, "My wife was three-months' pregnant and she was stabbed to death last year. Lost her and the baby." I just sighed. You never know the troubles people walk around with in New York.

—*Brooklyn Jury Warden Sharon Bierria*

Don't talk to the Po-Po (Police) and never give them your
government name.

>                                    —*A motto in a South Bronx project*

I didn't do anything. I'm innocent. I'm always innocent.

>           —*Louis Gross, an actor who plays a Mafia bodyguard*
>       *on* The Sopranos, *after being arrested May 1, 2006,*
>                    *for busting down his landlord's door*

A Queens man on trial for trying to kill his ex-wife's husband
committed suicide yesterday by jumping in front of a subway
train—the same day a psychologist was due to testify that he was
too mentally ill to be responsible for his 2004 crime.

>                —*Perry Chiaramonte and Jennifer Fermino*

In the name of freedom, barriers were raised throughout the city. In these times, however, security has become the ace of trumps. Few passengers complained and the normally feisty and independent New Yorkers not only lined up gladly to have their bags searched, but many went out of their way to volunteer to be searched.

—*Billy Gorta*

After working twenty-one years for this city in a compassionate and moral, responsible way—and making one mistake—I take very, very much offense that I was referred to as a "perp."

—*Former NYPD cop Earl Jones, to the judge who was sentencing him to jail for a DWI offense*

Boston King, an escaped slave from South Carolina, saw American slave owners, "seizing upon their slaves in the streets of New York, or even dragging them out of their beds."

—*Jill Lepore*

# THE ART OF BEING A NEW YORKER

New Yorkers, myself included, famously forget there's a world out there.

*—Thomas Oliphant*

It's New York City. It's rush hour. It is not time to jump off buildings.

*—Timothy Donohue, a building manager of the Empire State Building, on stopping a jumper on April 27, 2006, from the building's Observation Deck*

New York is the world's most successful example of group therapy.

*—Robert Zimmerman*

It's a sin to go to bed on the same day you get up.

*—New York City Mayor Jimmy Walker in 1932*

As only New Yorkers know, if you can get through the twilight, you'll live through the night.

—*Dorothy Parker*

From 1800 until approximately the Nixon era, it was universally acknowledged that the best bars in the world were found in New York hotels. . . . For guys who worked at these places, mixing drinks was a calling.

—*David Wondrich*

No longer do we yearn to quit New York. We are not drawn away. We are content to remain in New York.

—*Paul Rosenfeld*

New York is a city of right angles and tough, damaged people.

—*Pete Hamill*

[Maybe] even native New Yorkers felt like a tourist in (Times) Square, dwarfed, wanting to look up and read the electric headlines as they marched around and around....he had forgotten what it was like to be a part of New York. He had no particular urge to learn.

—*Stephen King*

Stitches for Snitches

—*T-shirt seen worn on a young man*
*in Harlem in the summer of 2005*

All the tough guys in New York are either dead or in prison.

—*Louis Cino*

You'd think New York people was all wise; but no, they can't get a
chance to learn. Everything's too compressed.

—*O. Henry*

A New Yorker is like every other American—only more so.

—*Mike Connor*

It's a city where everyone mutinies, but no one deserts.

—*Harry Hershfield*

New York is a place where the rich walk, the poor drive Cadillacs,
and beggars die of malnutrition with thousands of dollars hidden in
their mattresses.

—*Duke Ellington*

How is it possible that in the smartest city in the world, New York, that as a professional working woman, men still call me "Hon"?
—*Fran Napoli*

I have discovered that to be a successful New Yorker you must always be in a state of rage, just a quarter degree from overboiling.
—*Cynthia Heimel*

There are only the pursued, the pursuing, the busy, and the tired.
—*F. Scott Fitzgerald*

The hardest thing to be in New York is a nobody, and the town is full of them. The blind, the broke, and the beaten. Nobodies. They count too.

—*Charlie LeDuff*

New York—when civilization falls apart, remember we were way ahead of you.

—*David Letterman*

Children walking with their grandmothers talking foreign languages, that is the nature of this city.

—*Grace Paley*

New Yorkers preferred to keep their slaves, like their real estate and movables, in the family.

—*Jill Lepore*

Growing up in 1970s New York, Times Square was the Mecca for every degenerate east of the Mississippi.

—*Joseph Rogan*

New Yorkers talk as a nervous habit, the way people drum their fingers on the table, they talk because silence makes them uneasy.

—*Garrison Keillor*

New Yorkers are a ravenous people. Every hundred feet is a restaurant, coffee shop, or a frozen yogurt stand . . .

—*Garrison Keillor*

The New York play-goer is a child of nature, and he has an honest
and wholesome regard of whatever is atrocious in art.

—*Frank Moore Colby*

My dad was the town drunk. Most of the time that's not so bad;
but New York City?

—*Henny Youngman*

New Yorkers are mostly interested in New York—in case you
haven't noticed.

—*Jim Harrison*

New Yorkers do not deny the city's unlivability; indeed, they insist on it, wear it as a badge of honor.

—*James Nuechterlein*

Practically everybody in New York has half a mind to write a book—and does.

—*Groucho Marx*

New York is the meeting place of peoples, the only city where you can hardly find a typical American.

—*Djuna Barnes*

Every person on the streets of New York is a type. The city is one big theater where everyone is on display.

—*Jerry Rubin*

New York has more hermits than will be found in all the forests, mountains, and deserts of the United States.

—*Simeon Strunksky*

New York—that unnatural city where everyone is an exile—none more so than the American.

—*Charlotte Perkins Gilman*

New Yorkers don't make any contact with each other. They're either lost in their iPods, talking on their cell phones, or just crazy—talking to no one at all.

—*Robert Gonzalez*

New York is the biggest open air asylum in the world.

—*Anthony Volpe*

Everybody in New York is looking for something. Once in awhile somebody finds it.

—*Donald E. Westlake*

That overbalanced poise that makes the Manhattan gentleman so
delightfully small in his greatness.

—*O. Henry*

I love the impatience of New York. You ever had somebody not ask
you for directions, but demand them?

—*Jim Gaffigan*

In New York, we think it's appropriate to cuss more.

—*Amanda Christiansen*

Mother I am cursed—I'm a soldier when soldiers aren't in favor.
*—Sergeant Thomas Oathart on the Vietnam*
*Memorial Letter Wall off Water St., New York*

The voice was grouchy and harsh. If New York could talk it would
sound like Lou Stillman, who died this week at eighty-two.
*—Jimmy Cannon*

When I walk around watching New Yorkers like I do, they appear as
carelessly thrown together as a poor person's stew . . . maybe not too
tasty, but very colorful and interesting to look at.
*—Ernie Koy*

I'm not always that polite. I am just another New Yorker.
                    —*Nicholas Gray, owner of Gray's Papaya*

New Yorkers are known to throw things on the field at Yankee
Stadium. . . . At times they boo their mayor at parades. Some people
refuse to surrender their seats to pregnant women on the subways.
                    —*Winnie Hu*

I never bought any furniture in New York. For a year or so I lived in
other people's apartments.
                    —*Joan Didion*

There are only two classes in New York—the rich and the poor.

—*Fran Napoli*

New Yorkers are a street people whose lives are dominated by the daily human interactions on the city's sidewalks.

—*Vincent J. Cannato*

Immigrants who worked in the restaurants and garment factories of New York tended to live frugally and send most of their earnings home.

—*Patrick Radden Keefe*

I began to recognize that New York City was really a modern
Babylon, the melting point for peoples from all over the world.

—*Bernardo Vega*

The brotherhood that ran all through the Police Department was
very deep, and caused by a number of things, but one of them
was this, that it bound all of us up in the lives we had in this city.

—*Robert Daly*

If you want a rug seller, get an Arab. If you want a cop, get
an Irishman.

—*Jimmy Breslin*

You are a New Yorker when what was there before is more real and solid than what is there now.

—*Colson Whitehead*

I think there are more ghosts in the City than almost anywhere else . . . more people were attached to this City in life.

—*Rock Kenyon*

The firefighters were saying, everyday, who's going to do it if we don't, if the bravest don't, who else is going to risk death to save strangers?

—*Martin Amis*

Everyone in New York knows he is an important person living among other important persons.

—*Brendan Behan*

What is a New Yorker? Think about it for even a moment and you'll realize the answer is a moving target.

—*Gregg Stebben*

Not everybody on the subway is demented.

—*Michael Leapman*

Being born in New York is like a birthmark on your heart that leaves its stain on your soul for the rest of your life.

—*Fran Napoli*

The outdoors is what you have to pass through to get from your apartment to a taxicab.

—*Fran Lebowitz*

Meditation for most New Yorkers is thinking about their next apartment, the bigger one.

—*William L. Hamilton*

Maybe we become New Yorkers the day we realize that New York will go on without us.

—*Colson Whitehead*

The city is thronged with strangers, and everything wears an aspect
of intense life.

*—Edgar Allan Poe*

New Yorkers, even the most convinced cockneys, know little
of their city . . .

*—James Huneker*

I really believe that if they sent them to hell they would put it out.
The World Trade Center collapse was worse than hell.

*—Russell Best on the New York City firefighters*

Of all my parents' friends, the only one happy going to work was
a member of 120 Truck. I was only sixteen then, but that is when I
decided I wanted to be a fireman.

—*Peter J. Ganci Jr., Chief of Dept. FDNY*

It's hard to imagine that New Yorkers are willing to brave the subway
and a bus ride for much, but the promise of great food in an up and
coming neighborhood is a powerful motivator.

—*Andrea Strong*

As much as people who don't live here like to disparage New York,
and New Yorkers . . . they really do look on us with a great deal
of envy.

—*Mike Vaccaro*

[There] was a period after 9/11 when the city seemed like a city of neighbors, not a city of strangers.

—*Scott Heifernan*

There are New York snobs who love to beat up Broadway audiences almost as much as they love to beat up on Broadway shows.

—*Jim Schachter*

I am the accumulated memory and waistline of the dead restaurants of New York.

—*Bob Hershorn*

"Any evil intention against my cats and me will come back to you, three times." Thus spoke the witch of Elmhurst . . . casting a protective spell over her coven of cats—thirty strong.

—*Corey Kilgannon*

I LOVE IMMIGRANT NY!

—*Sign for immigration demonstration held in New York City on May 1, 2006*

[In] truth there was no posse left . . . all the Puerto Ricans had long ago sold their religious shops and hightailed it back to the island.

—*Amy Sohn*

With the network executives it was threats to your security and
kudos to your ego. . . . But I learned that game on the corner of
Chauncey St. in Brooklyn when I was a kid.

*—Jackie Gleason*

The best thing about the homeless in New York is that they are the
eyes and ears of the street. They help the cops solve more crimes
than any other kind of eyewitness.

*—Nina Kurtz*

Getting hired at the *Times* had an almost magical ability to turn young
people into young fogies . . .

*—Howell Raines*

After 9/11, I dreamed of joining the CIA!

—*Erica Jong*

In New York, sure. We're half the city. But upstate the only place you'll find more blacks than whites is Attica.

—*Chris Rock*

When I came out of my mother, right away, if anything happened in a three-block radius, I was a suspect.

—*Chris Rock*

The chosen were relieved that they did not have to beg for
invitation, hide their heads in shame, or invent excuses to
leave New York.

> —*Deborah Davis on Truman Capote's*
> *infamous 1966 Black and White Ball*

Can you imagine a modern-day New York hotel bartender smiling
when you order a Manhattan, asking which kind of bitters and which
kind of rye you'd like . . .

> —*David Wondrich*

A guy walked into the bar. He asked for a glass of water and started
talking everyone's ear off. You don't talk anyone's ear off at New
York's San Domenico. . . . Sure it's a bar . . .

> —*David Granger*

I'm a real city kid. To me, a pigeon is wildlife.

—*Nina Malkin*

The worn wayfaring men. . . . With the hunched and humble shoulders, Throw their laughter into toil.

—*Carl Sandburg,"Subways"*

Pig Foot Mary . . . began selling her steamed pig feet, hog maws, and chitterlings from a baby carriage on West 60th Street . . .

—*Linda Tarrant-Reid*

the newyork faces push into air: spilling into 42nd Street and Broadway—a scattered defeated army.

—*John Rechy*

We are like a bunch of spiders crying / but without the tears . . .
> —*Robert Lowell, from* New York Poems. *Lowell died in a NYC cab in 1977 on his way to the airport*

People's faces in Wall Street look fearfully gaunt and desperate.
> —*George Templeton Strong*

Philosophy, according to my optimistic friend, naturally inhabits the tenements. The people who live there come to look upon death in a different way from the rest of us—they do not take it as hard.
> —*Jacob Riis*

The docks were also crowded with people going to tashlich, and the lakes at Central Park. . . . But the true women of piety preferred to walk many blocks to throw their sins into the river.

—*Abraham Cahan*

No clothing too showy or too expensive, no jewelry too rare. Broadway is the place for him, the fine cafes and rich hotel lobbies.

—*Theodore Dreiser*

In the glittering gossamer of its fantastic buildings, tens of thousands of gray people, like patches on the ragged clothes of a beggar, creep along with weary faces and colorless eyes.

—*Maxim Gorky*

And she wept, "God bless you!" for the apples and the pears, And we gave her all our money but our subway fares.

—*Edna St. Vincent Millay*

Don Hedger had lived for four years on the top floor of an old house on the south side of Washington Square, and no one ever disturbed him.

—*Willa Cather*

For in the city, things were very definitely outside you, apart from you; you were definitely over here, they very definitely over there.

—*Paul Rosenfeld*

After all, every one in the great caravanserai of New York is a transient. . . . I am a transient of New York at night . . .

—*Stephen Graham*

As I walk up Broadway, the people that brush past me seem always hastening toward a destination they never reach.

—*Helen Keller*

Most young men who dwell in obscure studios in New York have had a beginning, come out of something, have somewhere a hometown, a family, a paternal roof.

—*Willa Cather*

To be born in the street means to wander all your life, to be free.
It means accident and incident, drama, movement. It means above
all dream.

*—Henry Miller*

Native New Yorkers are the best mannered people in America; they
never speak out of turn in saloons, because they have experience in
group etiquette.

*—A. J. Liebling*

His mama named him Marvel, but after a month on Lenox Avenue,
he changed all that to Jelly.

*—Zora Neale Hurston*

The citizens of New York are tolerant not only from disposition but from necessity.

—*E. B. White*

We were of the city, but somehow not in it.

—*Alfred Kazin*

Each tenement was a village square; each had its group of women all in black, sitting on stools and boxes and doing more than gossip.

—*Mario Puzo*

Our City can kick your city's ass.

—*Mayor Rudy Giuliani*

# Selected Works Cited

Allen, Woody, *Side Effects*, New York: Ballantine, 1981.

Baker, Kevin, *Strivers Row*, New York: HarperCollins, 2006.

Barton, Emily, *Brookland*, New York: Farrar, Straus, and Giroux, 2005.

Block, Lawrence, editor, *Manhattan Noir*, New York: Akashic Press, 2006.

Cannato, Vincent J., *The Ungovernable City*, New York: Basic Books, 2001.

Cantwell, Mary, *Manhattan When I Was Young*, New York: Penguin Books, 1996.

Deyo, L. B. and David Leibowitz, *Invisible Frontier*, New York: Three Rivers Press, 2003.

Ellis, Edward Robb, *The Epic of New York City*, New York: Coward-McCann, 1966.

Fairstein, Linda, *Entombed*, New York: Scribner, 2005.

Flaherty, Joe, *Tin Wife*, New York: Simon & Schuster, 1983.

Grain, Sara, *Dope*, New York: Penguin Group, 2006.

Hayes, Edward and Susan Lehman, *Mouthpiece*, New York: Broadway, 2006.

Janowitz, Tama, *Area Code 212*, New York: St. Martin's Press, 2002.

Lait, Jack and Lee Mortimer, *New York: Confidential*, New York: Dell, 1951.

LeDuff, Charlie, *Work and Other Sins*, New York: Penguin Group, 1996.

Lepore, Jill, *New York Burning*, New York: Knopf, 2005.

Lopate, Phillip, editor, *Writing New York*, New York: Washington Square Press, 1998.

McDonald, Brian, *My Father's Gun*, New York: Penguin Group, 1999.

McLoughlin, Tim, editor, *Brooklyn Noir*, New York: Akashic Press, 2004.

McLoughlin, Tim, editor, *Brooklyn Noir II*, New York: Akashic Press, 2005.

*New York, New York*, New York: MOMA, 2001.

Oliphant, Thomas, *Praying for Gil Hodges*, New York: Thomas Dunne Books, 2005.

Tosches, Nick, *King of the Jews*, New York: HarperCollins, 2005.

I would also like to thank and credit various editions and archives of *The New York Post*, *The Daily News*, *The New York Times*, *The New Yorker* magazine, *New York Magazine*, *Gotham Magazine*, *GQ* magazine, *Metro NY*, and *The New York Sun*.

# INDEX